nobody's mother

nobody's mother

LIFE WITHOUT KIDS

EDITED BY **LYNNE VAN LUVEN**
FOREWORD BY **SHELAGH ROGERS**

VICTORIA • VANCOUVER • CALGARY

Copyright © 2006 Lynne Van Luven
First edition

All rights reserved. No part of this publication may be reproduced, stored in a retrieval system, or transmitted in any form or by any means — electronic, mechanical, audio recording, or otherwise — without the written permission of the publisher or a photocopying licence from Access Copyright, Toronto, Canada.

TouchWood Editions
#108–17665 66A Avenue   PO Box 468
Surrey, BC V3S 2A7   Custer, WA
www.touchwoodeditions.com   98240-0468

LIBRARY AND ARCHIVES CANADA CATALOGUING IN PUBLICATION
Nobody's Mother: life without kids / edited by Lynne Van Luven.

ISBN 13: 978-1-894898-40-9
ISBN 10: 1-894898-40-0

1. Childlessness. I. Van Luven, Lynne
HQ759.N63 2006   306.87   C2006-905340-5

LIBRARY OF CONGRESS CONTROL NUMBER: 2006907469

Edited by Marlyn Horsdal
Book design and layout by Jacqui Thomas
Cover image by James Pauls/iStockphoto

Printed and bound in Canada by Friesens

TouchWood Editions acknowledges the financial support for its publishing program from the Government of Canada through the Book Publishing Industry Development Program (BPIDP), Canada Council for the Arts, and the province of British Columbia through the British Columbia Arts Council and the Book Publishing Tax Credit.

This book has been produced on 100% post-consumer recycled paper, processed chlorine free and printed with vegetable-based dyes.

foreword

I HAVE JUST TURNED 50 AS I WRITE THIS. There are a lot of things I feel I am grasping at last: being comfortable in my own skin, beginning to feel oddly sexy at a time when Germaine Greer says women become invisible to society. I am excited about what the next act will bring. There's some mystery to it. But one thing I know for sure: it will not bring children I bear myself. And finally, I am happy with that. But it has taken a while.

The first flush of baby-love rose up in me like a primordial swell when I was in my late 20s. It seemed to arrive overnight. I felt I was swimming in that lake where women down through the ages had swum. And I needed to find a mate. (It really wasn't quite that clinical but, looking back on it now, I see it as if not an imperative, at least some kind of directive.)

As so often happens, as soon as I stopped consciously searching, I found "the guy." If I'd had a list at the time, every box would have been checked off. He looked like Gary Cooper, he loved Mozart and Bessie Smith, he was a writer, he played hockey, he was funny (worked on the *Harvard Lampoon*!). He wrote me a letter a day for years, even when I was in the next room.

But it didn't work out with him. And just as that fact was sinking in, I had days on end when I felt fatigued, nauseated, headachey, sick to my stomach, when I had pelvic pain. And then I missed a period. I went back to him and said, "Hey, I'm pregnant," like some film-noir heroine in a last-ditch attempt to keep her man from slipping away. It didn't change his mind about us. I felt angry and sad and decided not to continue with the pregnancy.

It turned out I wasn't pregnant at all. What was growing in there were some advancing cervical cancer cells. I had the surgery and "poof," they were gone. After that, it was six-month rounds of (can we talk, sister?!) pap smears and cone biopsies. I was told I might not have been the best candidate to have children anyway because I had a severely prolapsed uterus.

Prolapsed. That was the word. It described exactly how I felt, as though I had fallen or slipped out of place, like my uterus. And just as I was trying to deal with this, all of a sudden almost every woman I knew was having a baby. I was happy for them. I had to be. They seemed focused, serene, fulfilled. As their worlds became smaller, their hearts became larger. Even if they were exhausted, they seemed to glow. And they were swimming in that lake I wanted to swim in, where women could just look at each other with a deep, shared understanding that they were all part of a chain of life.

I felt very unhappy for myself. I wanted in, and for a lot of reasons, I was out. No partner, bad physical prognosis, demanding job which I let consume me. Despite my outward mantle of success, I was sick at heart. And I didn't deal with it very well. Believing I had nothing to offer them beyond my imagining of motherhood, I withdrew from some of my oldest child-bearing friends. I was openly jealous of my sister, a new mom with a different, more profound relationship with our mom. So I got to be a failure on a number of fronts: as a woman, sister and friend. And for years, I wallowed in it.

But gradually, the wave of baby-desire receded.

Then I got together with the man I would eventually marry. He already had children: one son in his 20s, a daughter in her mid-teens and a son who was 10. I felt The Wave coming back. I wanted a child of our own.

My husband felt he already had a family, and indeed he did. I remember talking to him about the extraordinary measures I would go to, to have a child. And he would have to reverse a vasectomy. But it wasn't going to happen. I was so frustrated and hurt to recognize this last chance eluding me that I picked up a salt cellar and hurled it into a wall. It made a perfect, cellar-like indentation—a mark of my anger that I refused to cover up.

I started to work on a relationship with my husband's kids. It took us some time to get used to each other. I knew I wasn't going to step into a mothering role with them. They had (and have) a perfectly lovely woman who is, in fact, their mother. At first, I thought I would be lucky if we could be sort-of friends. It was a rough couple of years, mostly because I tried too hard to do things for them and was sickeningly nice. Fortunately, I couldn't keep it up; the more human I became, the more we started to communicate. I never, however, felt at all maternal—more fraternal than anything.

We have all warmed up to each other. I can say without reservation that I love them and I am grateful to have them in my life.

But I will always wonder (and now my younger friends are having babies and raising children): have I missed out on one of the greatest experiences a woman can have? Are mothers happier? Or just a different kind of happy? Are they more fulfilled? More topped-up as humans? Maybe the answers, whatever they may be, lie ahead in these pages.

℘ Shelagh Rogers
Gabriola Island, B.C., 2006

Shelagh Rogers is known for more than two decades of contributions to CBC Radio. Her voice, and that marvellous laugh of hers, is most recently heard weekdays on *Sounds Like Canada*. She is the recipient of the John Drainie Award for Outstanding Contributions to Canadian Broadcasting. In 2002, Rogers received an honorary doctorate from the University of Western Ontario.

introduction

WOMEN WITHOUT KIDS COME FROM ALL CLASSES, races, places and points of view. They are not, in fact, very much different from anyone else—except for that one little procreational detail, a detail with huge ramifications. Liberated people living in democracies like to think theirs is a pluralistic culture in which adults make individual choices, "do their own thing." And yet, every now and then, women without children realize that they are still viewed in some circles with suspicion, disdain or, perhaps worst of all, pity. *What are they up to, really, and what do they do with all that time when they are not raising children?*

I suppose I have been thinking about the Children Question one way or another for most of my life, as have many of the contributors to *Nobody's Mother.* I have had my fill of sitting mute at lunches and dinners while women around me talk on about their children's successes and foibles. About three years ago, I began asking other childless women to comment, frankly, about being childless, to explore how they think and feel about this particular aspect of their lives. The result of that quest is the book you are holding in your hand, a collection of personal essays written by Canadian and American women who range in age from their early 30s to mid-70s. Not all of the 21 contributors are professional writers—some are teachers, researchers, Aboriginal-rights activists and world travellers—although almost all of them rely upon language and the written word in their work. Some of them identify themselves as Second- or Third-Wave feminists; others deny any association whatsoever with the "F-word." Unlike me, some of them did not read Simone de Beauvoir's *The Second Sex* in their early teens. I read it in paperback because it was there, in my parents' high bookshelf. I read it hoping for, well, something sexy. Instead, what I found was even better: a French woman I had never heard of, voicing my own doubts about womanhood, someone who rejected motherhood because she "wanted to have only chosen relationships with chosen people."

All of the essayists in this collection have one thing in common: all have thought long and hard about the importance of motherhood, about their own skills and talents, about their own destinies and what "mothering" involves in North American society. They are aware that their choices have far-reaching and irrevocable consequences for them, their families and their larger communities.

Down through history, the phrase "mother and child" has always carried an almost incandescent power. It has been a force for the betterment of society—and it has also evoked images and feelings that can be easily exploited for monetary, political or religious ends. Perhaps worst of all, motherhood lends itself to an iconic idea about which people can be sentimental while simultaneously accepting terrible societal inequities, including homeless children, the sexualization of childhood and grossly inadequate daycare programs.

Is it any surprise that, as women's options grew over the last century, many felt less bound to the role of motherhood? Despite North America's media hype about "yummy mummies" and celebrity pregnancies, statistics show that childlessness is an increasingly common—and not always lamented—state. Statistics Canada's 2001 General Social Survey showed that one in 10 single women had no intention of taking on the role of mother; overall, 7 percent of women and 8 percent of men said they intended to remain childless. A recent survey showed that 33 percent of high-achieving North American women are still childless at 40. One American writer has estimated that as many as 20 percent of women in the United States are "childless by choice." And a dropping birth rate concerns politicians and demographers in many First World countries.

This collection of personal essays examines the child-bearing choice intelligently and honestly, from individual contributors' points of view; the essayists are your neighbours, your sisters, your colleagues and your friends. Not one of them is a nobody simply because she is "nobody's mother."

ℒ Lynne Van Luven
Victoria, B.C., 2006

the right decision

MARIA COFFEY

I WAS STUCK ON A TINY DESERT ISLET, out in Mexico's Sea of Cortez, with my husband, Dag. The Baja mainland was only a few miles away and we had a flight to catch, but for three days, a relentless northerly wind had been bearing down like a giant's breath, churning the ocean into a mess of whitecaps. Big surf pounded the beach with such vigour we felt the reverberations from each dumping wave. There wasn't a scrap of shade on the islet. Windblown sand scoured our skin and filled our ears. We were almost out of water. Our food supplies had dwindled to a small bag of currants, a cup of rice and some powdered milk. This, I kept reminding myself, was an adventure.

It was 1989, I was 37, and we were on our first overseas kayaking trip. Over the past two and a half weeks we'd meandered along the shores of a remote archipelago off the east coast of the Baja Peninsula. This was some years before kayaking boomed in the Sea of Cortez; apart from brief encounters with one other paddler, a few yachties in a sailboat and the occasional fisherman in a *panga*, we had had the islands to ourselves. As we paddled, glinting dolphins leapt into the sunlight ahead of our bow, fish skipped over the surface of the ocean in pursuit of prey and pelicans dropped beak-first from the sky in kamikaze dives. We explored beaches strewn with shark vertebrae and came across abandoned villages where we searched for old wells to replenish our water supply. We spent hours snorkelling, mesmerized by elegant moray eels, sinuous barracuda and iridescent parrotfish nibbling on coral. At night we cooked simple meals over small mesquite fires, feeding scraps to the tiny kangaroo mouse that scampered around our feet. Then we lay back and gazed at the planetarium sky, counting the falling stars. Tired by sun and exercise, we slept soundly with nothing to disturb us.

At times the isolation unnerved me, but Dag was in his element. For him, this was a beginning: he wanted to go on longer trips, in more remote areas. We'd started to talk about taking a year's sabbatical from our jobs and heading off around the world. Coincidentally, we'd also been talking about the possibility of having a child. Three years earlier, when I met Dag, he told me that he'd always imagined having a family—a large one. The idea had filled me with utter panic, and it still did.

Only once before had I considered getting pregnant, with a mountain climber who spent half his life away in the Himalayas on dangerous expeditions, who was far from ready to commit himself to me, or to a family. It was a ridiculous proposition, but passion overruled logic. It was also a short-lived dream. A few years into our relationship he was killed while trying to climb a new route on Everest. His body still lies on the mountain, close to its summit.

The moment I learned of his death, I understood that there was no way to defend oneself against such pain, except not to love so deeply. For years, love to me meant loss. And love was shadowed by fear. I developed separation anxiety, a condition Dag and I struggled with during the first few years of our marriage. Sometimes, when he was walking out of the door on a simple errand, I would cling to him in tears, convinced I'd never see him again. At airport farewells, I was an utter mess. If I was like that with a partner, what would I be like with a child? Wringing my hands every time he or she climbed a tree or rode away on a bike? I knew those kinds of parents, and I didn't want to turn into one myself. Dag understood my fears but assured me he would be a good balance. And when I watched him with other people's children, as he made them laugh like crazy, emboldening them to do things they never imagined they'd do, I thought maybe he was right.

Early on the fourth morning of our desert-islet sojourn, something unfamiliar woke us. The tent walls weren't shaking. The ground wasn't reverberating. The wind was taking a breather. Dag poked his head out and looked at the sky and the high clouds scudding south. "It's building again," he said. "But let's make a break for it."

After a flurry of packing in the dark we were off, paddling like fury toward the serrated sandstone escarpments on the mainland. The sun peeked over the mountains, turning them mauve, pink, red and gold. And the wind picked up, blowing hard on our nose. For an hour we moved like a machine, leaning into the paddling, hardly exchanging a word.

"How are you feeling?" Dag eventually called to me, from the back cockpit of the kayak. Without breaking my rhythm, I called back that I was longing to get to shore, eat a big meal, drink cold beer and wash the salt and sand off my body.

"Really?" He told me how sad he was that the trip was over, how much he looked forward to being out in the wilds again. "Even if we do start a family," he added, "we could easily have a baby along on a trip like this."

I stopped paddling. I swung around to face him.

"A *baby*? Are you out of your mind?"

"Why not?" He looked genuinely puzzled.

"Oh, just a few little things like baking heat, no shade, running out of food and water," I retorted.

"No problem!" he replied cheerfully. "You could breastfeed it. And anyway, babies are tougher than you think."

My response to that is unprintable. It began a furious "You don't know what you're talking about and never will!" calibre of row that, had we been at home, might have resulted in me slamming the door and threatening to leave Dag forever. But we were out at sea, stuck in a kayak, fighting not only with each other but with the wind and the waves that were now washing across the decks. We raged at each other most of the way to Puerto Escondido. There, tempered by a steak dinner and several beers, we made up. And we made some decisions. The first was to take that sabbatical and go off on a year-long, world-wide kayaking trip. The other was to shelve the baby discussion until we got back home.

᪐ "We travel most," writes Pico Iyer, "... when we stumble, and we stumble most when we come to places of poverty and need." During our long trip I stumbled again and again. The journey took us to far-flung places where life was as different to mine as I could possibly imagine. The people I met—especially the women—changed the way I thought about everything, especially myself. And they left me pondering the wisdom of dragging a kayak around the world instead of being home and having children.

On the shores of Santa Isabel, one of the Solomon Islands in the South Pacific, I fell into conversation with some women while I was washing my pots alongside them at the communal standpipe. Foreigners were a rarity in their village, and there was much gossip about the two strangers who had fetched up on the beach in a red boat.

"Is it true that you left all your children at home?" asked one woman.

When I told her that I had no children, she stared at me, aghast, the pot she'd been scrubbing hanging limply in her hand.

"No children! Why not?"

The reasons seemed too complicated to explain, so I simply shrugged.

The woman made sympathetic clucking noises. "What about your *wantoks*?"

Wantok, or one-talk, is a term meaning relatives, close friends and everyone comprising an extended family. In the Solomons, you have great obligations to your *wantoks*; if they need something that you have, you must provide it. I told her about my two brothers, living far away from me in England and Ireland, and my six nieces and nephews. This seemed to cheer her greatly.

"I have five children," she told me. "But only three are with me. My sister is barren like you, so I gave her my two youngest. You must ask your *wantoks* to help you."

Barren. It was how most of the women I met saw me. It was how I began to see myself. A vast, empty swath of land, where nothing flourished, like the flood plain of India's River Ganges. We spent six weeks there, inching our way through the maze of channels that the great river shrinks to during the post-monsoon season. Ironically, it was here that my fear of loss—the main reason I'd balked at becoming a mother—began to diminish. Paddling past floating bodies, seeing countless cremations along the riverbanks, stepping ashore next to human skeletons, witnessing a dog eating the body of a young girl: initially these seemed terrible things, but soon we came to acknowledge them as part of the cycle of life and death on the Ganges. For the first time, Dag and I talked to each other about our own deaths. If one of us perished on this part of our trip, we agreed, we wanted to be burned atop a pile of dung and wood, our ashes put into the river. The possibility wasn't too remote: banditry was rife along the river, and we'd already been chased by a man with a gun. The Ganges flood plain was the harshest place we'd ever travelled, yet it was bringing us the richest experiences of our lives. We lived in the encampments of saddhus, holy men who told us we were on a pilgrimage, that the sacred river would protect us. We were invited to stay in villages where the women treated me like a sister. They fussed over me, dressing me in their best saris, oiling my hair, putting bangles on my wrists and a red mark on my forehead to denote my marital status. Then, inevitably, they took me to their temples and made offerings to the gods, asking that I might return to them with a baby in my arms.

From India we flew straight to Malawi, in East Africa, and set off to kayak the length of its huge lake. The culture shock was extreme, but some things were familiar. One morning, I sat on the doorstep of a mud hut, next to a woman who was also called Maria, listening to the low insistent wailing of the grieving mother inside. The night before, Maria whispered, the woman's baby had died. He was her seventh child, and the third she'd lost to malaria. Later, the family would bury him with his siblings, in the shade of a giant baobab tree. It was a common story in Malawi, where malaria and AIDS rampaged. I sat there feeling desperately sorry for the woman in the house, for Maria and all her neighbours. They couldn't stop having babies. They couldn't stop them dying. They were trapped by poverty; this village was the start and end of their lives. I felt guilty about my freedoms and privileges, gifts these women couldn't begin to imagine. Then Maria leaned over and asked me how many children I had.

"No children," I said.

"Oooooh," she gasped, her face clouding with renewed sadness. "I am so sorry for you."

I adore newborn babies. I especially love the vulnerable spot on the tops of their heads, and the way it smells. I love it when I hold a baby, and it reaches out and pats my face with its tiny hand. I remember being on a rusty old ferry in Vietnam, the first time Dag and I travelled there in 1994. We were the only foreigners on the boat. Across from us sat a family group, playing cards. One woman had a little baby with her, adorably dressed in a silk outfit with a mandarin collar. When I smiled, the mother smiled back, then reached across the aisle with the baby and placed her in my arms. At first the infant took fright and started to wail. The young mother laughed merrily, took her daughter back, kissed her until she stopped crying and then offered her to me again. This time the baby gave me a gummy smile. For almost an hour I held her happily, sniffing her head from time to time, while her mother got on with her card game.

Not long after we got home from Vietnam, I was standing in line at a checkout desk in our local supermarket. Strapped onto the shopping cart in front of me was a bucket chair with a young baby in it. When we made eye contact, the baby chuckled and started windmilling his legs and arms. I forgot where I was. Leaning down, I cooed at him and touched his soft cheek. Suddenly the cart was yanked forward. Alarmed by the motion, the baby started to cry. I looked up and met the mother's angry gaze.

What did she think? That I was going to snatch her baby and run out of the store? That I had some awful, communicable disease?

"I'm sure she was worried about both of those things," said a friend I talked to later, who had a child of her own. "But I can't say I blame her not wanting you to touch the baby." She began to rail about the old ladies who used to lean over her daughter's pushchair, making comments about her plump, rosy cheeks. "Sometimes they'd even pinch her cheeks," she said. "It made me furious. It was so disrespectful. I mean, how would you feel if a stranger came up and did that to you?"

At first I thought she was joking. But no, apparently I had infringed the dignity of that child in the supermarket. And it wasn't just my friend who thought so. This trend in thought reached a nadir in 2004 when, in England, a hospital banned visitors from cooing at newborn babies. In a newspaper report, the hospital's neonatal manager was quoted as saying, "Cooing should be a thing of the past ... We often get visitors wandering over to peer into cots, but people sometimes touch or talk about the baby like they would if they were examining tins in a supermarket, and that should not happen."

My fear of loss was replaced by concern about having a child in a society of paranoid parents. But, as I edged into my 40s, we'd still not made the Baby Decision. Clearly, as long as I was still fertile, it would remain a possibility. I wondered how Dag would cope with the impact on our lives. He claimed that a child would slide effortlessly into our semi-nomadic existence. He held up as examples some friends of ours in England who also loved to travel. They had just had a baby and claimed they would tote him, and the siblings they planned for him, around the world. No problem! Babies, they agreed with Dag, are tougher than you think.

Almost a year later, we went to visit them. We arrived at their house just as they were about to feed their son, who was being introduced to solid foods. He was strapped into a small chair that was fixed on the edge of the kitchen table. Newspapers were spread all over the floor around him. On either side of the boy were our friends, each with a bowl and spoon in hand, taking turns to coax some mush into their son's mouth. We soon realized the need for the newspapers, as he spat out most of the food or, reaching his fat little fingers into his mouth, flung it across the room with impressive strength. In between mouthfuls he wailed furiously, drowning out any attempts at conversation. I stood back, watching this odd tableau—the angry baby, the food flying about, the adoring parents. And Dag, transfixed, gazing in horror at his friends, his role models in not-letting-babies-rule-your-life-or-change-you-in-any-way. We soon learned that all their travel plans had dissolved—as had Dag's desire to have a child.

Two years later, we were at home, getting ready to kayak around the Brooks Peninsula, a hunk of mountainous land that sticks out from the northwest coast of Vancouver Island like a giant thumb, attracting high winds, big seas and some atrocious weather. I couldn't concentrate on our preparations; I had missed two periods in a row, and was convinced I was pregnant. I went to the drugstore to buy a pregnancy-test kit. I had been to that pharmacy a thousand times before, but this was the first time that I had walked through the store via the baby paraphernalia aisle. I don't know how I got there. All I remember is standing, dazed, between shelves stacked with diapers. I stared wonderingly at the various packages: why had I never realized what an array of diapers there was to choose from? Then I noticed the people shopping around me—women with babies or toddlers in tow, a couple of them heavily pregnant. And all of them significantly younger than I. I thought, or maybe I spoke out loud because some of the women gave me strange looks, "I'm 45, which means that when this baby is 15 years old I'll be..." As I did the math I felt instantly sick.

When the test was negative, my relief told me everything. I didn't need a child to complete my life. I was happy being barren. And if I needed the love of children around me, there were places I could find it. I remembered the day in Malawi, after I left the house of the grieving woman and returned to our campsite by the lake. Some children followed me. They picked nuts from a tree, broke them open and taught me how to suck off the tart, sherbet-like coating from the seeds. The boys showed off with handstands and somersaults while the girls stroked my hair and picked through it, looking for lice. I didn't know who they belonged to and it didn't matter; here, in India, in the Solomon Islands, in Vietnam, children flowed in and out of houses and between families. Older children looked after smaller ones. Tiny girls toted babies around on their hips. An aged grandmother would offer a wailing baby her breast, for comfort. The lines between who could give love to children and receive it from them were blurred. So, on the shores of Lake Malawi, no one was worried about the strange white woman playing tag with some kids, pretending to be a crocodile and trying to grab them as they ran by, squealing in delight.

$\mathscr{L}$ Sometimes I wonder what it will be like if I end up in old age without a husband or children to comfort me. Maybe I'll move to Vietnam. I'll rent a little room in the Old Quarter of Hanoi, on a street — I know just the place — where lots of children gather to play badminton in the evenings after dinner. I can sit on my step and watch them. When one of them trips up, I can rub her knee and kiss it better. Some kid is bound to be carrying a baby brother or sister I can offer to hold while he plays with his friends. I can coo at the baby and smell its head to my heart's content. And I'll think back to the River Ganges. The evening I gazed over its flood plain, reflecting on its paradoxes. The compelling beauty of the poorest villages. The rotting bodies in a river with the power of physical and spiritual purification. The generous fields of marigolds, improbable splashes of colour in the monochrome, barren landscape. I'll remember, too, the argument Dag and I once had out in the Sea of Cortez, and decide that perhaps he was right, but that the time and place, for us at least, was wrong.

Maria Coffey is an internationally published author of 11 books, many of which chronicle her worldwide adventures with her husband Dag. Her titles include *Three Moons in Vietnam: a Haphazard Journey by Boat and Bicycle*, *Sailing Back in Time: A Nostalgic Voyage On Canada's West Coast* and *A Lambing Season In Ireland: Tales of a Vet's Wife*. Her recent book *Where the Mountain Casts its Shadow: The Dark Side of Extreme Adventure* won the 2003 Jon Whyte Award for Mountain Literature and a 2004 National Outdoor Book Award.

the contract

NANCY BARON

THE DECISION WHETHER TO HAVE A CHILD is not always a decision. All through my adventure-filled 20s, I was not sure I wanted children. But then, at the age of 29, I met Ivan.

Ivan was an economist. From my perspective as a biologist, that seemed a staid profession. But Ivan was anything but dull. He spoke six languages and had lived and worked around the world. His Victorian house, with its vibrant green and coral walls, wildly painted furniture, folk art, artifacts and Afghani rugs, was an exhibit of his life. I teased him that his design style was "museum of anthropology." In the sitting room, a black-and-white photograph of Ivan astride a horse stared the viewer in the eye. Two fierce-looking Afghani tribesmen flanked him. But for his pale eyes beneath the turban, Ivan could have been one of them. For three years he had lived in Afghanistan as part of his research for his Ph.D. His Pashto was fluent, and his tales about the trade routes through the Hindu Kush and the forces that influenced them mesmerized me.

Ivan embodied self-sufficiency. He was resourceful and multifaceted, a man who landed lightly on his feet in every situation. In retrospect, I think I wanted to *be* Ivan. I admired his extreme self-confidence and

I wanted to extend my own outdoor adventures to work abroad. But by 1986, when we met as I was passing through Vancouver to go sea kayaking, he was already moving out of his far-flung phase. I didn't know it then, but as far as Ivan was concerned, his next venture would be parenthood.

Our long-distance courtship was short and very sweet. It included frequent flights between Banff and Vancouver, bicycling trips to Napa, California, and lengthy conversations as we explored each other and our views of the world. My biologist's instinct told me that Ivan was "fit," a survivor. He was a mate who would always provide, although that part mattered little to me because I'd been financially self-supporting since university. But Ivan had an effect on me: I was just plain crazy about him.

Sometimes, when I saw him from a distance, I would think, "My god, he looks like a used-car salesman." He would strut down the street, muscular but on the short side at five foot nine, wearing a flamboyant shirt he had designed for himself, dark aviator glasses, loafers with clickers on the heels, oozing his usual self-confidence. That would be my last coherent thought. As he approached me, it was as if he exuded an anaesthetic; I simply went under.

I loved Ivan's exuberance, his wide-ranging intellect and the energy with which he told a story. His clear blue eyes, sandy blond hair and toothy grin were attractive, but it was his energy that women and men alike found irresistible. I loved how he interjected dance steps into a walk to the store.

"Life is a celebration with you on my arm," he would sing, his arm linked through mine as his feet did a little soft-shoe step.

Ivan loved to dance. Early on in our courtship, he took me to Harbour Dance Centre in Vancouver. As a former aerobics instructor, I thought I could catch on, but the class was beyond me. It was filled with regulars, people who had danced for years. I thrashed along as best I could, thinking that at least my mortification would be over in an hour. But at the one-hour mark, I learned that the class was 90 minutes long, and the last half-hour was choreographed. I could have fled, but I decided I might as well go down in flames. Ivan danced with attitude; I spun like a top out of control, certain he must be appalled to know me.

But he surprised me. At the end of the class, he ran over and in front of everyone gave me a bear hug. "You are such a great sport," he said. I took up jazz dance.

After only six months of knowing Ivan, I left my job of five years as a biologist and naturalist in Banff and moved to Vancouver. I left behind not only my hard-won position with Parks Canada, but winters telemarking in the backcountry, summers hiking, canoeing and birdwatching. In an act symbolic perhaps of shedding my old life for a new one, I gave away most of my belongings, even those with sentimental value, and consigned the rest to a shop, never once checking back. I gave away most of my clothes too—didn't think my mainly fleece wardrobe would fit Ivan's lifestyle. My circle of close women friends wondered if I had taken leave of my senses. Sue, with whom I shared a cozy Parks house on Grizzly Street, discreetly saved a few special paintings and photos, suspecting I might want them again someday.

When I moved to Vancouver, Ivan proposed that we should live together on a trial basis for three months. During that time, either of us could change our minds—no hard feelings. It felt a bit contractual, but I viewed it as a challenge. I would win his lifelong devotion.

Living with Ivan was a new kind of adventure. He brought me lacy dresses from Bangkok. "Close your eyes," he would say. "Keep them closed."

He would outfit me in his latest vision of fashion, then tell me to look in the mirror. I found it hard sometimes not to laugh. One little number I recall had a snug-fitting bodice and a high neck with cutaway shoulders. Past my hips, the entire dress was see-through white lace falling in uneven layers. Surfer girl gone bridal, definitely not me, a tall, former tomboy/mountain girl. What would my friends from Banff think if they could see me in these getups? But I gamely wore them for Ivan.

Sometimes I would go along on business trips, and we would tack on a few days of exploring. While Ivan was helping set up the first shrimp farms in Thailand (which, I later realized, were an environmental debacle) for Canada's development agency, CIDA, I would slide off birdwatching. Up early, I struck off alone with my binoculars; upon my return, I would recount vivid tales of hornbills and howler monkeys. If I made it enticing enough, I thought, he might come with me. Ivan mocked "Nancy's desire to be in the bush," but he wasn't entirely resistant. One day I came home and found a bright red sea kayak, with a balloon attached, displayed on the altar of our marble dining-room table. No gift he ever gave me mattered more.

Within the three-month contract, Ivan made me a new offer. He was ready for a family, he said, and since he was already 40, 11 years older than me, he had no time to waste. He was prepared to marry me—if I was prepared to make having a family my priority. I recall his telephone conversation with his mother in Montreal.

"I've found the woman that I want to be the mother of my children," he told her.

I was just turning 30, a symbolically appropriate time. And I unequivocally wanted a life with Ivan.

Our wedding was a happy affair. I wore a grey silk tuxedo with diamonds and emeralds from Bangkok. I had my hair and makeup done. My friends were bewildered at the new cosmopolitan me.

On our wedding night, we officially began trying to get pregnant. Following my usual scientific method, I researched pregnancy. I bought a digital thermometer and recorded my daily temperatures, tracking ovulation. Each month I imagined I could detect early signs: tender breasts, a feeling of fullness. But each month my period appeared. The first drop of blood was the signal that sent my heart crashing. But as the months ticked by, it became the symbol of my failure. I could see it in Ivan's eyes. I could feel his angst growing.

After almost a year, the ever-resourceful Ivan suggested I see a famous gynecologist. Appointments were hard to come by and typically took a year and a half, but Ivan had connections. It hadn't been that long, the specialist said, but if we wanted to investigate, the first step was laparoscopy, a procedure in which a tiny camera is inserted through a small incision below the navel.

I remember coming out of the anaesthetic. In a dreamlike state, from very far away, I heard the verdict. One Fallopian tube was blocked; both were scarred and lacking the feathery cilia to wave the floating egg into the tube. It would be very difficult for any egg to find its way home. Heartsick, I imagined it—the egg careening off into the void, never finding its way to my waiting womb.

As I tried to comprehend what had gone wrong, I recalled a strange infection I had had at the age of 15, supposedly an offshoot of strep throat. The infection had been difficult to check; it had moved throughout my entire body, and I had been hospitalized for several weeks. When I told Ivan, his reaction shocked me. It was as if I had knowingly betrayed him. Why hadn't I disclosed this, he wanted to know. It had never occurred to me. But as the tension between us mounted, I began to feel guilty.

I was sad and depressed, but undaunted. We arranged for surgery to unblock my tube and to remove scar tissue. The abdominal surgery would require two weeks' bedrest, but this seemed like a small price for a child. I felt certain the situation had been sent to try me, but if I were determined enough, we would succeed. Memories of the surgery and what came afterwards are fragmented. I remember checking myself into the University of British Columbia hospital. Ivan paid me a cursory visit before the next morning's operation. It was a long, lonely evening.

My next clear memory was hearing the surgeon describe what an ordeal the surgery had been—for him.

"Eight hours I scraped away," he declared. "The scar tissue was as if someone had poured crazy glue over everything."

I stared at him. "Is there any hope?"

"Only time will tell," he said.

But I was running out of time. As soon as I was out of the hospital and back in my own bed, Ivan left on a business trip. I was shocked. "You aren't leaving right away?"

He was and he did. My friend Andy, who had also moved to Vancouver, played Florence Nightingale. He had been the captain of our Parks Canada Banff-Jasper Relay running team. We had become close pals, connected by our history. Andy came to see me each day, bringing pizza, groceries and good cheer.

I focused on healing. I read Shakti Gawain's *Creative Visualization* and imagined open tubes. I imagined my tiny but determined egg spinning though space to find its way to my now-spacious Fallopian tubes where it would embrace an eagerly waiting Ivan-sperm and migrate down into the uterus. I visualized pregnancy and a child and Ivan's joy. I imagined walking down the street with our child in a stroller as I identified bird calls for our junior naturalist-in-training. I thought about a reading list of my favourite childhood animal stories and sought out women who had had fertility problems but had succeeded against the odds.

"If it happened for them," I told myself, "it can happen for me."

Ivan's work trips became more frequent. At home, he became increasingly remote. He admitted he felt I had hidden my childhood infection and my potential infertility. He felt duped. And he was afraid. At 41, he believed he was running out of time. I pleaded with him: we could overcome this together, we could do in vitro and we could explore adoption. But he was unconvinced. In despair, I yelled at him: Didn't he love me for me? Was I simply the vessel for his child?

He was treating me as if he had made a bad purchase. I implored him to hang on, but he had lost faith. He made a half-hearted attempt to start the in vitro process in Seattle—the waiting list at UBC was too long. He wanted a child and he wanted it without all this grief.

On May 9, four days before my 32nd birthday, Ivan's secretary informed me he had decided to extend his three-week business trip to Africa with a two-week holiday in Thailand. He had sent me, she said, a cassette tape. I could pick it up at his office. I drove there, drove home and turned off the car. With fumbling fingers, I popped the cassette into the car's tapedeck.

Ivan's radio-announcer voice was shaking. I could hear the dryness of his mouth, his words clicking as he spoke: he wanted to end the marriage. It was the best thing for both of us. Our pain was tearing us apart. He had sent the tape so that that by the time he returned home, we would have begun our separate lives. He would move out temporarily and allow me to continue living in the house for three months while I decided what I wanted to do in my new life.

Listening to the tape, I felt flooded: sadness, resignation and even a drop of relief. At least I could stop the monthly anguish of trying to get pregnant. I walked into the house and threw the tape into a drawer. After sitting a long time in silence, I phoned Andy. I told him the end had come—by cassette tape.

"Ivan's greatest hits," he said dryly. I laughed through my tears.

For my three allocated months, I knocked around Ivan's museum of anthropology like the lost soul of one of the exhibits. I pored over photos of our good times together, proof of my former happiness. My lunch breaks consisted of long walks around the Stanley Park seawall, weeping, often in the company of my friend Élin, who worked with me at the Vancouver Aquarium. Evenings, I watched the sunset from the top-floor bedroom, alone.

Then suddenly, an opportunity came up to go to Borneo with a small group of conservationists. Since I was the only woman, I persuaded Élin to come. I suspect she would have done almost anything to end our seawall-wailing walks. On the plane, I accidentally left my journal in the seat pocket—and lost the detailed chronicle of my three years with Ivan. I was devastated. But the trip, difficult and occasionally dangerous, refocused my eyes on the wider world. Borneo, with its mud, mosquitoes and men with machine guns guarding sea turtles from poachers, reawakened my deep concern for nature under pressure.

Upon my return, I gradually rediscovered all the things I loved besides Ivan: birds, natural history, the ocean, wilderness and my work. And the greatest discovery of all—I once again found myself.

My obsession with motherhood receded into a distant blur. I could see a pregnant woman on the street without my heart lurching. Close friends had children, and I celebrated with them. I know that, for them, having a family is the most important thing in their lives. But I also see their sacrifices and the paths not taken. I know they envy me my freedom; I envy them their children—but would we trade places?

I soon met a man who shared my values and who told me he had no interest in having children. Years later, he reminded me of one of our early conversations: I had told him I had found and lost the love of my life.

"Really?" I asked. I realized I had left behind my all-consuming love for Ivan; it was gone, like my once-precious journal. My new love and I spent seven years together, leading ecotours (not always together) and exploring the natural world. Then we moved to Whistler. My partner needed a break from his ecotourism business and wanted to focus on building the house of his dreams. We grew apart; I became restless. I was still focused on work and trying to make a difference for Mother Earth, who I feel is straining to care for all of us.

In 2000, I moved to California for a new job. I now work with top marine scientists from around the world; we try to bring to light what is happening to the world's oceans and what it will take to restore ocean health. And I have a rich community of colleagues with a common cause. To my surprise, in my mid-40s, I found a soulmate, an American journalist who shares my passion for conserving what's left of the natural world. He, like me, never had children, and it is a tinge of regret we share. We live on 20 acres of avocado and citrus farm on the outskirts of Santa Barbara. Bobcats, coyotes, rabbits and road-runners roam our "yard," and we keep a running list of over 50 species sighted on our morning walks on the property with Fanny the dog.

Evenings, we watch the sun set over the Channel Islands. We listen to the coyote chorus and the great horned owls hooting. And, as we toast our good fortune, I realize that I owe Ivan a debt of gratitude.

Nancy Baron, a zoologist and science writer, now works in the United States as Ocean Science Outreach director for SeaWeb/COMPASS. From 1988 to 1995, she was the education director of the Vancouver Public Aquarium. Her field guide, *Birds of the Pacific Northwest*, was published in 1997. She's the winner of two Canadian Science in Society awards, a National Magazine Award and a Western Magazine Award for Science.

a woman without

LORNA CROZIER

THE FIRST THING TO NOTICE ABOUT THE CONDITION is that the words used to describe it are negative and denote a lessening or loss. The most common is "childless," followed by the thin-lipped phrase "a woman without children." That bears a disconcerting resemblance to a woman without a man, a woman without an ounce of common sense, a woman without a penny to her name. For years, I've tried to come up with an alternative. "Child-free" just doesn't cut it. The phrase sounds too much like "smoke-free" and might lead to the misconception that I find children toxic or at least, bad for your health. It's as if on my front door I've posted a photo of a child's head inside a red circle, a red diagonal slash superimposed across the face.

Fearing that I may be overstating the language issue, I look up childless in my handy *Roget's*. Surely I'm missing a synonym that I wouldn't mind wearing. In the index, there's only one number for childless, 166.4. The main heading under which the word falls is "unproductiveness." So far, not so good. I still hold out some hope, however, because Roget and his learned lexicographers list 43 synonyms. A quick glance shows they all have one thing in common: they're about as negative as you can get. "Barren, arid, gaunt, dry, dried-up, exhausted, drained, leached, sucked dry, wasted, fruitless, teemless..." the list goes on. One word that's new to me, "acarpous," sparks a moment of optimism until I check it out in *Webster's*—it's from the Greek and means "bearing no fruit, sterile."

Now, I come from farming country, where words like these are not taken lightly. I have to remind myself that I'm not researching the Dirty Thirties or flipping through descriptions of the prairies during the last several years of drought. I'm checking out the word childless. Suddenly I see myself as a vast stretch of land that's never felt a rainfall; the sloughs are dry, and alkali draws a thick circle of chalk where the water should be. The few scrub bushes are leafless, brittle and stunted. There's a grey farmhouse in the distance like the one in Andrew Wyeth's famous painting, windows boarded up, the roof caved in. Beside a tilting shed sits an old tractor, half-buried in a dome of dust. The wind blows over the broken field, sucking any colour from the earth, any hope from the human heart. This is the landscape of my body. This is the woman without.

Is it any wonder most people look at me with awkwardness and pity when they ask me about children and discover I am childless? A word brings a whole history with it, an alphabet of attitudes, a cultural reading that translates its dictionary definition into what it really means. Several of the other synonyms in the thesaurus's childless section begin with "un," the prefix that turns something into its opposite and usually affixes "the lack of" to the root word's meaning. "Unfertile, unprolific, unplowed, uncultivated." It doesn't seem to be stretching it to add "unloving" and "unloved."

Language becomes the most interesting at its points of fracture, those moments of tension and failure when all we mean to say can't be said. If you ask me, I'll tell you I am a woman who has no children, but I am not without, I am not less. Should I list, instead, all that I have and then decide if there's something missing? The available vocabulary calls me unproductive, wasted and dry-wombed, and I can't find one fit, fearless word to throw a punch and knock these bullies off the corner. There's no pleasing substitute for "childless" working its way from silence to the tip of my tongue.

Living outside of what we usually mean by "a family of one's own" is a complex state that evokes every emotion, including sadness and relief, so mixed together that any attempt at description reduces me to a sigh. Maybe that's because when we speak of a woman without children we're speaking of The Other, one of those who lives on the edge of what our language and culture feel comfortable with. If mother is one of the most powerful words in our mother tongue, what is its antonym? How do I speak of what is not-mother in the scanty vocabulary we have? How can I describe the day I stepped through the door marked "Those Without Children," and no alarm went off?

℘ In some ways I chose not to have children; in other ways, I didn't make that choice as much as it made me. Throughout my young adulthood, unlike many of my friends, I didn't go soft-eyed and giddy at the idea of holding a sweet-smelling bundle swathed in pastel woollens. There may be several reasons for that, including ones I'm not consciously aware of, but except for a few years in my mid-30s, I didn't long for a baby. I didn't feel any need to extend my genes into the future; there were enough humans in the world without my red-faced resemblances squalling into the light. Children were not a way of ensuring happiness or endowing my days with meaning. That hard task was mine alone.

I am, of course, my mother's daughter. She's proud of her two children and she takes the time to say so, but, good daughter that I tried to be when I lived at home, I could not erase her parents' cruelty; I could not protect her from my father's selfishness and drinking; I couldn't move her from the ratty little rented house where I grew up or pay her higher wages for the cleaning jobs she took on to make ends meet. I couldn't raise her self-esteem. And today, I can't make her less lonely as she spends another holiday by herself with a turkey and all the bounty that goes with it on a prairie table over a thousand kilometres away from where I now live on the west coast.

From the time I hit high school, I was a wound-up fury heading out the door, in love with words, with the plays we put on in the school gym, with the passion I was learning about in the back seat of a car. And though I did my best not to act like a "brain" in school, I was determined to get educated enough to break away from my small town and lead a self-sufficient female life free of my parents' poverty and my mother's dependence on my father, who was mean with money and with love. At university and during my first teaching job, my arms didn't ache from the absence of a baby. They ached from a pile of books and the weight of all the other things I tried to carry to make up for the cultural dearth of my childhood—Rilke's advice to a younger poet, Germaine Greer, good shoes, Bertolt Brecht, Cabernet Sauvignon, avocados and tall jars of olives, Bob Dylan, Yeats and Akhmatova, curries and rare roast beef, Ibsen and Bergman, freesia in the house in a milk-glass vase. My life without children did not feel empty. Nor does it now.

Admitting this sometimes makes me feel like a stranger among others of my gender. Recently at a dinner with six women, I was asked, as I often am, if I wished that I'd had children. From experience, I know the expected answer is "yes," or at least, "sometimes," but I responded with a question, "Do you wish you hadn't?" The woman I addressed said no. But she went on to say that a positive answer would have meant that she'd be wishing her present children out of existence. Would her response have been different if I'd worded the question another way? "Let's say your children are alive, but living happily and healthily with another family who loves them. Do you ever wish that you didn't have children?" This question is not asked as often as the one addressed to me. Everything in our culture assumes the lack is in my life, not in hers, the more common female path of children and grandchildren, the universal raison d'être for one's time on Earth.

Some women who, like me, have spent their working lives as teachers might have responded differently to my dinner companion's query. In similar situations, I've heard them say their students are their children; they don't need any others. Though I've been fond of many of my students and though they keep me connected with generations other than my own, they're not there to fulfill my maternal needs. I do my best to be a good teacher and mentor, but with one or two exceptions, they already have mothers, thank you very much. In our time together, which is relatively brief, it's my job to challenge them and care for them in a more detached way.

Others claim animals as their children. Again, that equation doesn't work for me. I feel squeamish when someone calls me the mother of my cats. I wouldn't mind even a small amount of their grace, quickness of eye and felicity of ear, but I don't have these feline qualities in my genes. The two cats who share my life are distinct creatures of another species. I adore them, perhaps too much, but they are not ersatz babies in the house. Nor are books, though they've been called a writer's children, especially if that writer is a woman without a family of her own. The metaphor is a thin rationalization for a condition that seems to need an apology or explanation. Surely there is no substitute for a daughter or a son. Either you have a child or you don't.

For a few years when I was in my mid-30s, a voice inside my body demanded "baby, baby, baby," but I was with a man who'd had five kids already and who'd had a vasectomy. Here's where choice becomes complex. I'd come nowhere near to wanting a child during the 10 years of my first marriage to a man who was good father material. I was busy getting an education, learning the art of poetry and inspiring my students, I'd hoped, with a love of literature. Now, when my body was driving me toward motherhood, I was with the wrong man. Was Patrick's refusal to have more children one of the unconscious reasons I'd chosen him? I could long for a child like a "normal" woman, weepily bemoan my fate and then blame him down the road if I thought my childlessness was a mistake. I wouldn't have to accept responsibility for my loss.

I felt no regrets at first. Our relationship was so intense and fraught with battles that I thought we wouldn't last more than a year, and my new life would begin. The choice would be mine all over again. I could have a child or not. That was 28 years ago. Patrick and I are still together, and I wouldn't give up one day of my life with him, even the difficult ones, for anything else the world might offer. Sometimes, however, I imagine the child who might have been; sometimes I see her in the shadows that are close to sleep. In the garden, with others of her kind, she is a flickering deep within the bamboo; she is moonlight pouring from the throats of lilies. Would she have made my life different? Yes. Better? I don't know, but my days are bountiful and rich even though I live without what children bring.

In "Living Day by Day," a poem I wrote in my late 30s, I tried to find words for my situation, one that is not less or empty though sometimes there's an ache in it, as if I almost hear a song my mother taught me, but the words are gone and only a faint, fractured melody remains.

> I have no children and he has five,
> three of them grown up, two with their mother.
> It didn't matter when I was thirty and we met.
> *There'll be no children*, he said, the first night
> we slept together and I didn't care,
> thought we wouldn't last anyway,
> he and I struggling to be the first
> to pack, the first one out the door.
> Once I made it to the car before him,
> locked him out. He jumped on the hood,

then kicked the headlights in.
Our friends said we'd kill each other
before the year was through.

Now it's ten years later.
Neither of us wants to leave.
We are at home with one another,
we are each other's home,
the voice in the doorway,
calling *Come in, come in,*
it's growing dark.

Still, I'm often asked if I have children.

Sometimes I answer yes.
Sometimes we have so much
we make another person.
I can feel her in the night
slip between us, tell my dreams
how she spent her day. *Good night,*
she says, *good night, little mother,*
and leaves before I waken.
Across the lawns she dances
in her white, white dress,
her dream hair flying.

🖎 A year or so after Patrick and I moved in together, I visited my mom in Swift Current, and we went for our usual morning walk. There was something important I had to tell her and I felt frightened. She has always struck me as the quintessential mother. All through my childhood, she'd had to work to keep us in groceries, but she wasn't what you'd call a career woman. Her jobs were difficult, low-paid and often demeaning. And her fierce love for her two children led me to think, in the self-centred way of offspring, that we were the centre of her life. As she and I climbed the steps to the overpass above the railway tracks, she told me that Patrick was good for me. She was glad I'd left my marriage and we'd found each other, although our running off together and the minor scandal it had created had upset her for a while.

"Mom," I said, the wind from the west making us lean slightly to the side, "I don't know if you realize this," I paused for a moment to catch my breath, "but if I stay with Patrick, I won't have children."

I waited for her to pull me to a stop, I waited for her wrath and disappointment to spin me around like the wind and drop me on the tracks below. I waited for her to tell me to leave him.

"Lorna," she said, "not every woman has to have children, you know."

I was stunned into silence, and we kept on walking side by side. She mentioned my cousin who'd had two kids and wasn't happy with motherhood. She said that God might have other plans for me. She told me she loved her children, but we were gone. Her life went on without us; we weren't what gave her days grace or value. What a gift she gave me almost 30 years ago, my mother saying as we crossed the overpass in the city where she gave birth to me, "Not every woman has to have children, you know."

❧ When I was a child visiting my maternal grandparents' farm on Sundays, I'd always volunteer to clean the chicken after it had been plucked and the pinfeathers singed over the fire that sparked and hissed from the open burner of the wood stove. I loved reaching inside the hen and pulling out the warm, slippery package of intestines, gizzard, heart, liver and sometimes, if I was lucky, a small necklace of eggs glowing in the light of the kitchen, each one blue-white, the colour of moonstones. I find it odd that human eggs are so much smaller; most of us have never seen them. Are they as beautiful, I wonder, magnified and held up to the light?

This spring I turned 58, far past child-bearing age. The uterus is the only organ in the human body that diminishes with time. Mine must be parchment-thin, a phantom part of me, the once-full pear-shaped purse emptied of its bright pearls. Whatever choice I had about giving birth is gone. Scientists say nature abhors a vacuum and something always moves in to fill the vacated space. Perhaps in me there's a new awareness of the fragility of life now that the possibility of reproduction is over. Perhaps there's a sharper sense of the thinness of time's membrane that separates me and those I love from whatever, if anything, lies beyond.

And where there's loss, is there more room to feel blessed for what exists? How lucky I am to have an 88-year-old mother to whom I talk on the phone every Sunday. How lucky I am to have poetry as a close companion and to have lived almost three decades with a man whose bones I want my bones to lie with in the earth. Do I regret not having children? First, let me say again that my life has not been a lessening, an acarpous stretch of wasteland like the one I see in my parents' old photos of the dust bowl. My life has been a gathering, not a giving up. Then, I'll answer yes; I'll answer no.

Lorna Crozier has taught at the University of Victoria since 1991. She has published 12 books of poetry, the most recent being *Apocrypha of Light* (2002). Her books have received the Governor General's Award, the Canadian Authors' Association Award, two Pat Lowther Awards for the best book of poetry by a Canadian woman, the Dorothy Livesay Award and the National Magazine Awards' Gold Medal. She has also published non-fiction in various anthologies and has edited several collections of essays. Her poems have been translated into several languages and she has read her work from one end of the world to another. Her love for animals, especially cats, is boundless.

a different
kind of calling

DIANNE MOIR

SILENCE FILLS THE NIGHT AIR. Stars spangle the black velvet of the Yukon sky. I am working with the Teslin First Nation this winter. Much of our collaboration has to be done in the evenings, as many of my group work during the day. After the meeting I walk along the highway back to my motel, accompanied by an Elder.

Suddenly, she asks me why I never married and had children; she calls me a nurturer. I feel a sudden loss, a strong feeling of failure: have I missed something really important in my life? A heavy, empty feeling washes over me in waves. I say nothing, choked up.

Then the old woman turns to me, takes both my hands into hers. "Of course," she says, "I understand. All of our communities that you help are your babies. You care for us, cry for us and take us by the hand and guide us. You are *one who brings change*."

I stand still, shocked—how did this woman know my traditional name?

I was born in 1948 to a northern Cree family of the Waskaganish First Nation. My mother was educated; her father had demanded that all 13 of his children go to school. My father was a credit to the "system." He was educated until he was needed by his father to help take care of his family. That was the rule until the Second World War, when my father joined the armed forces and sailed off to see the world. My mother and father married during the war, and I was born six years later.

I am the eldest of nine children, two girls and seven boys. The boys are actually cousins who were either partly or fully raised by my parents due to their own family situations. My grandmother, Gookum, was a powerful influence in our family. Her word was understood to spring from a woman of wisdom, spirituality and medicine. She delivered many of the Cree leadership of today and protected both young and old with the strength of her beliefs. She believed that all women must have children to fulfill their destiny. Children were the future of the nation.

When I was four, I was sent to residential school in Quebec. I stayed at L'Ecole de la Sacre Coeur until I was 14; I was sent back to my parents when I refused to become a member of the order. Becoming a nun had held some interest for me: that was almost all that I had known, but I did not have the "calling."

However, I did have wanderlust, and I was a pain in the butt. I never let a second go by without questioning my teachers about religion, world affairs, history and culture. (I think the nuns may have been relieved when I left.) I was the one who stole the communion wine for a friend's birthday celebration. I was the organizer of the St. Jean Baptiste Day "breakout," which was followed by a police chase. But I was also the one who was regularly locked in a closet for punishment—and was routinely told that I was a dirty savage and a heathen. I lived up to my reputation. However, I also remember the nuns running along the sidewalk and showing us how to slide after a freezing rainstorm, their black habits flying in the wind and their whoops of laughter challenging us all to best them in the adventure. They made learning a quest: never easy and never without twists and turns. They taught me to be flexible with myself and with others. These are memories that I often have to revisit. I was returned home to my parents a demanding, belligerent, self-serving brat.

As I did not speak English and my parents had moved to Toronto, I entered secondary school with a big chip on my shoulder. I looked for any reason to challenge. What I did not know was that my anger at being sent away disguised my hurt and strong feelings of abandonment.

Then came my first stroke of luck. I started a job with a residential mental-health facility. The staff there must have seen me as a walking outreach client, as they all supported my search for self-identity and self-worth. I worked on wards that were similar to those in Ken Kesey's *One Flew Over the Cuckoo's Nest*. It was exciting, foreign and yet comforting. Each day after shift I would sit on the streetcar going home and hold my ward keys, reminding myself that I was outside and able to move freely. Many of those who were in the hospital showed me how close we all are to simply stepping over the line and entering a different world.

When asked why I did not stay in nursing, I often joke that I only entered in order to find a rich doctor to take care of me for the rest of my life. But that is not true. The thought of marriage was so far out of my viewfinder that if I had met a candidate during those years, I probably would not have recognized him. But I was not without love affairs and wonderful romance, oh no. I loved the romance but did not want the responsibility.

About that time, my mother died suddenly in a car accident. My father fell apart; my sister, who had been in the car with my mother, was ill for some time. The responsibility for the family fell to me. I had to mother, support, guide, feed, clean up after and generally put everyone else first. Not a good time for this kind of sacrifice: I was 20 and working as a psychiatric assistant in a big city mental-health centre. I was on a roll: I was edgy, sexy and totally self-absorbed.

Those were also the days of the first modern land claims in Canada. Because I was in university, the older folks of my home community felt that I should be involved during the developmental stage of the discussions of the Northern Quebec–James Bay Agreement. The negotiations were heady, and they catered to my ego and my search for confirmation. I travelled with leaders, sat at the table with national politicians, dined with power brokers and was asked my opinion. Wow, I thought, I was dangerous.

When the dust settled, one of the chiefs decided that I should return to the reserve and get married. His reasoning was that if I was in the community, I would be available for cheap, if not free, consulting services. Yikes! I ran.

I ran as far west as I could imagine, to Edmonton. I hid out there, happily having marvellous monogamous relationships but not really looking for long-term connections. Oh yes, I felt the pressure of friends and couples around me. Sometimes it was really hard to balance my reality with the societal picture of what a woman should be. I found myself borrowing other people's children for weekends. I was fond of one in particular, Galen, known as Big G. We would go to ice shows, music festivals and movies, wander around town; he was a regular visitor and remains a favourite friend to this day. In many ways, Big G calmed my fears about not being a mother. He is in his 30s now and a happy guy.

Native organizations and communities in western Canada discovered my background and soon I had a successful consulting business. My job was to assist communities to deal with crisis situations, establish safety and direction toward health, and transfer the skills. What I found was disheartening. I saw people defining themselves as victims, based on their personal experiences. They were victims because they were forced to drink due to living conditions or poverty or isolation. They were victims because they had been in residential school and were not parented and so could not be expected to parent. They were victims because they stayed in abusive relationships or participated in abusive parenting patterns with their own children.

Over and over, I heard communities saying that children were their most precious gift and their most valued resource. I challenge that statement. If that were so, we would not see one, not one, abused or neglected, hungry or lost Aboriginal child. The community would have stepped in. But I also know that until the community says "Enough is enough," nothing can change. Throwing money at the problem will not help. Making professionals available will not help. Communities have to be ready: ready to work and to feel the pain of change. Those that are ready are a joy to work with. Moving on is sometimes really hard, as I have made friends and helped to create vision within some of these communities. Such work is rewarding and rich: the role of a woman who can bring change.

Who am I now? Well, I am not, and have never been, a rip-roaring feminist. That does not mean that I do not stand up for myself or feel that I cannot take care of myself now and in the future. I don't wear a bra because it is uncomfortable. I take care of my health but am not worried about a little weight gain or wrinkles. I love my grey hair. I have never carried a placard or marched against anything. I do believe that abortion should never be used as a birth-control device, but that there are occasions when it is medically (due to physical or mental health) necessary. I am a proud practising Catholic.

I learned recently that among Prairie Cree, "Woman who Brings Change" has another responsibility: she is the one to bring balance between the homosexual and heterosexual communities. I have never had an issue with homosexuals. The skills and wisdom that I have seen within their ranks are gifts that I treasure. To find balance between the two worlds? Well, that is a challenge.

I love my siblings' children. I dote on them. I loved them as babies and cherish my relationship with them as they move toward adulthood. Have I missed having children of my own? Not yet—but as I grow older and realize that I could be alone in my last years, community becomes increasingly important to me. Perhaps that will be the family of my golden years. Ultimately, being nobody's mother has allowed me to "mother" in less traditional ways. But then again, maybe that is the tradition of my foremothers and therefore my own destiny.

Dianne Moir was born to Frank Moir and Margaret Morrison in 1948. She connected to her James Bay Cree roots after she had finished her formal education (R.N., M.S.W.) and during the Northern Quebec/James Bay Agreement negotiations. Since then, she has assisted Aboriginal communities throughout Canada with governance development and healthy community growth planning. Having recently moved from Alberta to British Columbia, she continues to be connected to a wide group of blood and chosen family and friends.

half a
mother twice

BRONWEN WELCH

I SOMETIMES WONDER IF I FELL IN LOVE with my husband when he said he'd had a vasectomy. We were drinking cider at a local pub when he told me that he already had two children from a previous marriage and had no particular desire to have more. I think that was our second date. I thought his revelation was interesting (I had never known someone who had had a vasectomy), but I did not give his news a whole lot of my attention. Only about a year and a half later, when we were discussing the possibility of marriage, did I confront the idea that I would never have a child of my own.

I have now been married for four years. My husband is 48, 17 years older than I am. We both grew up on Vancouver Island, both have master's degrees in English literature and both teach English at our local community college. We have a lovely house and garden, wonderful friends. Because I am now 31, various friends and relations tell me that my biological clock should not simply be ticking—its alarm should be starting to ring. My clock, however, while it emits the occasional bleat, is pretty quiet. Its overall silence is due, in part, to the fact that my husband's daughter has lived with us for the past five years.

I love my stepdaughter, but five years ago, when Thea was 12, that love was arguably more a product of will than anything else; these days, it definitely operates in a more graceful capacity. Thea was pretty angry when I first began living with her father. A quiet, socially introverted child with a severe speech impediment, she had spent much of her childhood feeling both isolated and angry. Her parents' divorce understandably rocked the foundations of her world, and since she had a hard time making friends, she had very few people to whom she could relate. When I met her, she reminded me of a small wounded animal: desperately in need of unconditional love, but ready to lash out at people who might offer it to her. That first year with Thea taught me the value of patience. It also showed me that love does not always spring forth naturally like an artesian well; sometimes one must divine for it.

Now my relationship with Thea is stable and loving. We enjoy each other and share many activities. We love our house, and both of us are happy to putter around our kitchen, baking bread and listening to CBC Radio. Sometimes we sit quietly together in the kitchen (which we agree is the heart of the home), both reading our books and watching as the golden afternoon light fades to dusk outside a window framed by clematis vines. We love domestic tranquility; the sound of rain against a window and the smell of baking bread are, to us, the sound and the smell of peace and harmony.

A short time ago, while Thea and I were doing the dishes, I mentioned the prospect of my writing this article and the ambivalent feelings I have about not having my own child. She was understandably curious: "Why would you feel sad about not having your own child?" she asked. "You already have me, and I think I'm probably enough—why would you *want* any more?"

It was hard for me to explain to her that there is a small part of me that wonders how the love for my own, biological child might differ from the love I have for her. People are greedy for all kinds of experiences and all kinds of love. We live in a society that tells us we can and should have it all, and I am no different from anyone else. But how best to tell a child whom I love that sometimes I wonder if the love I feel for her might not be enough for me? So I told her the truth: that I have moments of sadness, moments when I wonder what my own child might look like. I explained that I sometimes feel like I might be missing out on one of life's ultimate, transformative experiences. She listened carefully, then responded by saying firmly, "Well, you should have a baby if you really want one." Her generosity never ceases to amaze me, and it is ultimately her love, and her acceptance of me and our relationship, that has made me realize that she *is* enough: more than enough.

Additionally, I can't help remembering that when I was her age, I was partially in charge of a sister four years younger than I was. My parents divorced when my brother was 12, I was 7 and my sister Annie was 3. Through some kind of unspoken agreement, I became Annie's third parent.

My quasi-parental role seemed fairly natural at the time. Through no one's fault, our childhood was somewhat chaotic. We lived one week with my mother and the next with my father, so every Sunday night we would pack our bags and prepare to move households. Moreover, the two houses that we gravitated between were wildly different in both character and appearance.

Once the divorce was finalized, my mother, who had always wanted to live a rural lifestyle, moved out to a portion of Vancouver Island quaintly called the Highlands. It is a 45-minute drive from Victoria, and, when we first moved there, was devoid of any of the usual trappings of civilization. We spent three years at the end of a dirt road in the middle of our 12-acre piece of property (which we named "Winter Creek") before my mother and stepfather could afford to install electricity or running water. The house (which they built with their own hands) had very little insulation. It took them years to be able to afford glass windows. On windy nights, the plastic on our bedroom windows flapped until it sounded like canvas sails on a ship at sea. The house was heated with an old wood stove that melted the bottoms of our school shoes when we rested our feet too close to it.

My stepfather, Cal, was bearded and gently scruffy. He favoured jean overalls and plaid shirts, as opposed to silk ties and business suits and, while my biological father, a university professor, was frequently reading or writing books and articles, my memories of my stepfather are of his cheerful whistling as he chopped wood. Cal was from Port Alberni, used the word "spuds" to describe potatoes, listened to Bobbie Gentry and drank his beer with tomato juice. I adored him.

In addition to my mother's three, Cal had two children from his previous marriage. Our house was always filled with kids, dogs and cats, and salamanders in empty cottage-cheese containers. My mother divided her time between launching her career as a potter, running a portable sawmill business with my stepfather and casually, but very lovingly, raising her family. My early memories of her are of a radiantly happy woman habitually clad in dusty jeans and liberally bedaubed with clay.

My father stayed in the original family home, located in a quietly upscale part of Victoria. The house, in which he still lives, is enormous, and copiously decorated with Oriental carpets and old books. He bought his daughters gowns (pink for me and blue for Annie) to wear specifically to the opera, and made French-style crepes every Sunday morning.

Every few years my father would remarry. Endlessly optimistic, he married three times after my mother, and in between his wives he had various other attachments. None of these women were bad people, but as soon as one relationship seemed to be permanent, it would come unglued, a process which always seemed to demand much screaming, swearing and slamming of doors.

My little sister clung to me in those days as one of her only points of stability. My father, while devoted to his children, was also devoted to his academic career, and quite often left me in charge of my sister, since my brother had already left home. (My mother, when we were not at her house, wholeheartedly pursued her career as potter/portable sawmill owner/operator.)

I remember the fear I used to feel taking the bus home from school with Annie. The school, chosen by my parents for its progressive program, was an hour by bus away from my father's home. By the time I was nine, I could successfully navigate Annie (age five) and myself downtown, where we would transfer by crossing two busy streets to catch another bus that would take us into our neighbourhood.

I was perpetually panic-stricken about somehow misplacing or losing sight of Annie and clutched her frantically during the entire journey. I didn't understand that there were many buses, and if we missed one, another would be on its way soon. I was always anxious about failing to catch what I believed to be our only chance of transportation and would hurry Annie relentlessly off one bus and onto another.

Once we got home, it could be several hours before my father arrived, and I would try to entertain Annie while starting dinner as well. Since I was only nine, my patience would often wane. However, any anger or impatience I expressed toward my little sister in those days I would later bitterly repent.

Consequently, I feel as if I have already experienced many aspects of motherhood with my sister. I regret all the times I was impatient with her and pushed her away from me when I became tired of her company. I wake up grief-stricken about the time I wouldn't share my Halloween candy with her, or the time I scared her by pretending I had rabies. Perhaps there are many sisters who frighten their younger siblings by pretending to froth at the mouth, but I doubt any of them feel as guilty about it as I do.

Annie started going off the tracks when she was 13. Unlike my brother and me, she wasn't satisfied with her status of social misfit and all-round dweeb. She started a desperate campaign to become cool. No one in my family, I should add, has ever been cool. It was an impossible standard for Annie to achieve; she was trying to break out of a genetic mould that had been set in stone for generations. Yet, she discovered that high school kids are impressed by grittiness, by people who don't seem to care about the world or themselves, so she began to go over the edge as a way to gain super-cool status.

On her 14th birthday, I found her passed out on her bed, covered in regurgitated lime Jell-O and vodka. She was also soaking wet. I never told either of my parents because I believed that they couldn't handle the truth. I continued my silence as she dropped acid, smoked, shoplifted and stole money from my father's wallet. Eventually she left high school for good when she was 15.

Terrible fights became common as Annie grew older. Finally she refused to spend any time at my mother's home. She considered it the "boonies," too far away from her motley assortment of friends, so in town she stayed. My father's life now consisted of screaming arguments, late-night phone calls from strange young men and an angry teenage daughter who would often not return home until early morning.

At a certain point in her early teens, Annie took savage delight in describing her first sexual experience to me. Had I been a normal older sister, I am quite sure I would have behaved differently than I did. But I had lost sight of what regular sisters did. Looking back, I think my sister desperately needed me to be normal; the last thing she wanted me to do was weep over her lost innocence, which is exactly what I did: huge, melodramatic, embarrassing tears while we waited to see how the pregnancy test turned out. I now realize that I should have shrugged and allowed her to carry on with the process of growing up.

By the time Annie was 19, she had become a heroin addict and was willing to do a great deal to support her habit. She cut off all ties with her family and disappeared from our lives for months at a time. Occasionally she would call me to tell me she had been evicted from her apartment, or that her most recent boyfriend had kicked her out. Then she would camp on my couch until she found somewhere else to live. We tried living together once, but I recognized it as an unmitigated disaster after she unintentionally set fire to my kitchen. When Annie stayed at my apartment, I would try to sneak glimpses of the child she had once been, the child I had loved. I found that when she slept, she regained the round-faced innocence that had been hers when she was eight.

Thea is the polar opposite of Annie. At 17 she has completely puritanical attitudes toward alcohol and spends her weekends volunteering at a retirement home and a local thrift store. She wears her long brown hair in a neat ponytail and favours heavy-knit sweaters and buttoned-down shirts instead of plunging necklines. Her favourite class is photography; on her holidays she reads library books and bakes cookies. She once made a thousand paper cranes. As I write, she is knitting scarves to sell at my mother's annual Christmas craft fair. She knows far more about world politics than I do. I often wonder if she is normal.

And yet, I have some of the same fears for Thea that I once had for Annie. I watch her sometimes, when she is knitting or reading a book, and I think, "How can I keep you safe?" "How can I protect you from beginning that all-too-short journey toward feeling that you are worthless?" So I try always to tell her that she is beautiful, and that she has important ideas to share with the world. I try to listen to her when she speaks to me, and I consciously try to return her hugs with lots of enthusiasm. But most of all, what I try to do (and the operative word is try) is to relax, to let her relax: to give us both a little breathing room. So when she retreats into silent anger, doesn't study for tests or forgets to phone when she is going to be late coming home from school, while my first reaction is frantic worry that she is heading for a life on the streets, my second reaction is simply to allow her a bit of space.

I tell myself that I am more capable than I was when I was nine, but I am still pretty young to be doing this job, and I trust myself less now than I did 22 years ago. People, I have discovered, need a fair amount of air to flourish; hovering, on the other hand, does tend to stunt growth.

I dream sometimes that I am hurtling along the road in an old car without seatbelts or brakes, and that both Annie and Thea are in the back seat. Although Annie is much better these days, and has made huge strides toward ending her cycle of addictive and destructive behaviours, I still occasionally wake up in my warm, comfortable home to wonder where she is and what she is doing. Is she, for instance, passed out somewhere on the street or, worse yet, going home with someone to whom I would merely give spare change? Her chaotic lifestyle and our mutual confusion over our unusual relationship have precluded much communication in recent years, but she is never far from my thoughts. I love her, but I sometimes wish I did not. The particular burden of love I feel for Annie is completely parental in nature: a smothering, all-encompassing desire to protect her at all costs. I feel imprisoned by my love for her, and this feeling is no different now than when I was nine years old; it confuses me just as much now as it did then.

In short, I feel my stint in the world of parenting is coming to a close. I am pleased to say that I feel no urge to ask my husband to reverse his vasectomy. I am happy with what we have. I have my books and my home, my cat, my friends, my family, my garden and my new career. Perhaps most important of all, I have Thea. I would be lying if I said I didn't feel wistful now that several of my friends are mothers, but I firmly believe that my own maternal energies are almost tapped out. Babies turn into teenagers, and teenagers turn into adults, and I don't think I can watch that process again, quite frankly. I have been half a mother twice and I think that is about all I can handle: I simply don't have the energy for anything else. Maybe this isn't the way I would have planned my life, had I been in charge of the cosmos. My life may seem unusual, but I have the sneaking suspicion there is no such thing as a normal life. In the end, this *is* my life, and I am happy.

Bronwen Welch was born and raised in Victoria, B.C. She has a master's degree in English from the University of Victoria and teaches both English literature and composition at Camosun College. One of her most satisfying activities is puttering in the kitchen with her stepdaughter Thea. She also derives great satisfaction from "working insanely" in her garden.

no child of mine

KATHERINE GORDON

I'M 42 YEARS OLD. I HAVE NO CHILDREN. I'm very happy.

But you would be so much happier if you did have a child.
Excuse me?
Children are such a joy. Having one would make you really happy.
I'm sorry. I know you mean well. But what makes you think you know what makes me happy?
You're not complete unless you have children.
Ah. A person cannot be whole without kids? And therefore cannot be happy?
That's right. You don't know what you're missing.
Well, I can't argue with that. But I could say the same of you, of course.
You don't have to be defensive, you know. It's not too late. You have options. You have choices.
I made my choice a long time ago.

It isn't an accident or for lack of potential fathers that I have no children. It's by design. In the court of public opinion, however, I am judged a misguided woman; someone who has foregone a fundamental experience essential to life fulfillment. How can you be complete if you have not procreated? This is wrong; you must be persuaded to change your mind. Certainly, you cannot possibly be happy.

Don't you like your friends' kids?

Sure. I even love some of them. I especially like being an aunt.

Then surely you want one of your own!

Nope. For me, parenthood makes no sense at all.

What kind of person are you, not wanting to be a mom?

Someone who makes parents uncomfortable to be around, I guess — the unhappy ones, anyway. To justify their decision to include children in their lives, parents have to judge me by their own standards and find me wanting. To dispel any discomfort they may have at being parents, they tell me what they believe I really think and feel, even when they do not know me at all. Either I have made a poor choice:

You don't know what you're missing.

Or I am in denial:

Every woman really wants a child, whether she admits it or not.

Perhaps I am simply not telling the truth, from shame:

Poor thing, she can't have children but she doesn't want to say.

But the truth is much simpler than that. I have no interest in being a mother.

You've never had the slightest doubt?

Nothing's ever black and white, of course. I have always said that while I can't envisage ever having a child, perhaps I might change my mind one day. But in truth, that's just a pacifying statement to keep people at bay. I have never once yearned to be a mother. Remaining childless has not even been a conscious decision-making process. There have been no long, agonizing nights wondering whether I have made the right decision. No uncertainty has plagued me.

You're so selfish!

That's an odd way to describe me, I think, but let's see. Let's say my reasons for being childless are entirely selfish (however, I think that word means something different to me than it does to you. I think of it being more related to self-ness). To me, my childlessness is a state of being, like the colour of my skin. It's the nature of my self, if you like. My hair is dark, my eyes are grey, I'm five foot six; I have no children. Those facts all fit comfortably into the same sentence; they are part of who I am and was born. Other unchangeable self-ness: I'm half-French, half-English, a youngest child. Culturally, I'm a New Zealander, even after living in Canada for more than a dozen years. You could add any number of other characteristics: I'm a runner, but I like trails, not city streets. I like to travel; I favour the remoteness of Patagonia or Alaska. I love the ocean. I cannot live away from it. That's just the way I am.

But—don't you want to share those things with children?
No, I don't. I do not want to share my adventures with a child. I want to experience them for myself, perhaps with other adults.

I do not want to be interrupted. I do not want to change diapers, or think about babysitters, or pay school tuition. I do not want to hand my car keys over to a 16-year-old. I do not want to worry about a child late home from school; I do not ever want to know what it must feel like to lose one. I do not want to be held hostage to parenthood.

You're going to be a lonely old woman. Who's going to look after you in your old age?
I can't get very worked up about that one. I have seen many lonely old people who have children. I think I'll rely on my friends.

My kids will look after me in my old age. It's all in how you bring them up.
I hope so, for your sake. But the world has changed; children leave. The old people may not get put on ice floes any more, but there's rarely room in the igloo for them these days.

Don't do it.
What?

Don't do it. We love our kids, of course. But if we had known how hard it was going to be, we wouldn't have had kids. Really, don't do it.

Wow. Thanks for your honesty. That doesn't happen often. Most parents who think that way would never admit it. Of course, I can see how hard it is, and I know I don't want to experience what you've gone through.

Don't listen to those people saying it's hard. Really, it is such a joy to have children. We just want you to experience that joy, too.

I know you do. That's because you don't understand how joyful it is not to have them. Some parents really do have an overwhelming desire for me to understand the pleasure of having children: they cannot fathom an existence without them. And friends, of course, don't criticize. They listen to my reasons with respect, if not understanding. Strangers are another matter. Boundaries of respect vanish when the issue of children — or lack of them — comes up in conversation.

♫ Do you have any children?

I know you don't mean to be rude, so I suppose I don't mind you asking (although it's not a question I am going to ask you). The answer is no.

Are you planning to have any?

Of course that's your business: silly me to be offended. Um — no, actually.

Why not?

Should I just laugh and say I forgot, or tell you the truth? Because if I tell you to mind your own business — well, you're just going to think I'm the rude one. If I lied and said I couldn't have any, would you be embarrassed? If I tell you they don't interest me, how will you respond? Children are such a joy, after all: why wouldn't everyone have them if they could? Why wouldn't everyone want to talk about them?

You'll be a dried-up, empty old woman if you never have children.

Acceptance that childlessness lends itself to a rich, rewarding and positive existence would upset the precarious premise upon which many parents have accepted the negative consequences of having children. (There aren't many who are openly in the "don't-do-it" category.) The accepted belief is that it is only by having children that one can have a rich existence. Perhaps denouncing my status, loudly and often, somehow justifies being a parent.

That isn't a very forgiving analysis, I know. But why else are so many people so perpetually insistent that I should change my mind? Friends see the wealth of my existence for what it is, I suppose, while strangers have not had the opportunity. But the assumption that I am incomplete in some way by someone who does not know me, and that they think they know me better than I know myself, simply astounds me.

You'll change your mind. You'll feel quite different when you have one of your own.

I guess we'll never know, will we?

Don't you realize how much children make you part of a community?
Ah—the you're-the-odd-one-out argument. Not having children is an affront to accepted societal and economic standards. Childlessness must therefore be questioned by society and, if possible, corrected. It is a state outside the norm, in a world where we all want normality. Hence the primal urge to make me see the error of my ways, regardless of the irrationality of the argument.

Make sure you have your babies before you get too old. You need to plan them, you know.
Excuse me. I thought you were my doctor, not my life coach.

Systemic assumptions and intolerance also exist. Want paid time off work to have a baby? No problem. Want a few months of unpaid leave to undertake some other meaningful personal project? Forget it. There are no financial grants to people who have refrained from adding the weight of more children to already overburdened school and health systems. No tax breaks that say, "Well done, you, for not having kids."

Give me a break. What right have you got to complain?
Actually, I'm not complaining. I'm just calling a spade a spade.

I am a realist. I know these attitudes won't change. I can live with that. What needs to change are societal attitudes toward having children. It isn't selfish to refrain from breeding: it's the opposite. What would you call procreating simply to indulge a desire to recreate myself in my own image? Or having a child to look after me in my old age? How selfish is it to add another environmentally disastrous human being to an already overpopulated globe?

Oh come on, you're exaggerating.
You think so?

People are not gentle on the Earth, let alone on each other. There's no guarantee that I would produce a smart, compassionate, environmentally responsible individual who would contribute positively to society. Even if I did, it's a scary world we're leaving as a legacy for the next generation. I like to think I'm wrong—about the planet, that is. There are good reasons to think there is a positive future. I'm frequently convinced there is one in store. But all my other reasons for not being a parent still stand.

We're thrilled to announce the birth of Teresa May, nine pounds two ounces, with blue eyes and dark brown hair.
That's wonderful! I am so happy for you both! I can't wait to see her.

I really am happy for new parents, agog with ecstasy over their newborn. Babies are beautiful. Their parents' joy is tangible, if not infectious. I don't think they are wrong, or irresponsible, to have taken on parenthood. In fact, their hope and inherent optimism cheer me immensely. I may not be interested in being a parent, but I am interested in people. Today's children are part of my future; they are the people on whose shoulders all our hopes will ride eventually.

It would be nice, in fact, to think that other people's babies will one day be agents of change to a more compassionate society in which people's individual choices are respected, and their differences celebrated. A world where a childless woman is not seen as something "less" but as someone who is whole.

I'm 42 years old. I have no children.
I am very happy.

Katherine Gordon, born in England, has been travelling the world since she was three months old. After living in New Zealand, South America and Costa Rica, she moved to Canada in 1989 and now lives on Gabriola Island. She has worked in Aboriginal treaty negotiations and commercial law. She has published a number of articles and books, including *A Curious Life: The Biography of Princess Peggy Abkhazi* and *The Slocan: portrait of a valley*. Her most recent book is *Made to Measure: A History of Land Surveying in British Columbia*.

sometimes i feel like a childless mother

LAUREL BERNARD

I'VE NEVER WORRIED ABOUT BEING CHILDLESS. When people ask if John and I have children, my main feeling is: "Are you mad? Have you looked at us closely? Would you trust us with children?" Still, thinking about it, I realize I'm slightly embarrassed by the question. There's this impulse to explain, perhaps carry a card:

> YES, I AM CHILDLESS. NO, WE HAVEN'T BEEN TRYING. AND NO, I AM NOT TRAGICALLY BARREN. YES, WE HAVE A HOUSE AND JOBS AND COULD BE BRINGING UP CHILDREN, BUT THIS DOESN'T MEAN WE'RE EITHER BON-VIVANT SWINGERS OR CHILD-HATING YUPPIES. NO, PLEASE DON'T THINK HOW NICE IT MUST BE TO HAVE LOTS OF DISPOSABLE INCOME, A MARTHA STEWART HOME AND UNLIMITED FREE TIME. WE HAVE NONE OF THESE THINGS. YES, WE HAVE PETS, BUT WE DO NOT REGARD THEM AS CHILDREN. YOU WILL NOT HAVE TO LOOK AT THEIR PICTURES; I DO NOT CARRY WALLET-SIZE SNAPS. WE ARE REASONABLY EASYGOING, NORMAL PEOPLE, JUST LIKE YOU. WELL, EXCEPT FOR THIS CARD.
>
> — LAUREL

After that, if I dig down, there's a sense of—what is it? Wait, yes, I am a woman—guilt. Obviously, there must be something wrong with me. Why don't I have children? Should I have had them? Why didn't it ever come up? Other couples seem to make actual decisions about child-bearing. I just let us go gently into that "Good night, I'm too tired to talk" phase. And now, at over 50, I have to wonder: do I regret not having children?

These are meaning-of-life questions, issues of immortality that have troubled philosophers throughout the ages—so I need to make a list. I'm sure this is the way Socrates, if he'd had MS Word and no friends, would have done it.

Why don't I have children?

1. Well, for a start, I never made a list.

2. I'm writing a book so I don't have time. This would be a great excuse if it were not for the member of my writing group who has— very inconsiderately—managed to complete and sell two novels on top of mothering a tribe of children and pets.

3. John and I are eccentrics who prefer animals. I would deny this, but it's true; we once had three cats and a dog in our 1,100-square-foot home and now it looks like the set for Amityville Horror 3: Curse of the Demonic Claw-Beings. We also spent hundreds of hours creating a website for Sadie, our dog, plus matching T-shirts. And we shot, edited and packaged a mock-training video of her. And, even though she's now dead, I've modelled the dog in my book on her, written three articles about her and can't seem to get through any piece of writing without mentioning . . . oh.

4. I have no maternal instinct. No, both John and I like children. Although not exactly because they're children. I like what they like— animals, games, Harry Potter—while adults have an inexplicable fascination with golf, gardening, home improvement and those strips of patterned paper that go around the top of rooms. At social occasions, I'm the one trailing the family cat because, if you can get hold of them,

cats are warm and furry, and they purr. As for John, he's the one over by the scented candle, surreptitiously melting his swizzle stick into zigzags.

5. Let's face it: we don't have children because we *are* children.

Why did it never come up?

1. No positive reinforcement. Perhaps couples want children if they remember themselves as cute, loving kids who were a pleasure to bring up. My childhood memories are of terrified caretakers dragging me away from high trees, weed-infested ponds where you could drown and strangle at the same time, and railway tracks. For several preteen years I travelled London by Underground or rode on the back of a motorcycle owned by my guardian, whose interest in children—as I later found out—was more akin to Lewis Carroll's than Dr. Spock's.

2. No experience of family. People must lean toward children if their own childhood experience of family life was happy, or at least intense. (As I grow older, I realize experience doesn't have to be pleasant for you to want to repeat it; we cling harder to our neuroses than our dreams.) My childhood was memorable—Dr. Sacks meets Dr. Seuss, perhaps—but a family experience? No. Most of it was spent among children in a British boarding school, an experience not designed to foster family values, unless your idea of family is *Lord of the Flies.*

Should I have had children?

1. I once watched a man in a coffee shop telling his young son stories about his life. I heard the lad say, "But weren't you frightened!?" And, seeing that look of pure trust and admiration, I thought: "Why, of course—you can lie to children! If they're young enough, they won't remember."

2. Obviously not.

Do I regret not having children?

1. Sometimes. It is touching the way children want to hear about you

and what you've done. My writing group is interested in my life—sure—but only so they can suck the story ideas out of it. Never trust writers. Those long nights awake, that pale and hungry look—that's not because of hours spent in front of a screen; it's because they're vampires. One moment you'll be sharing a convivial glass of wine, and the next, you're Lorena, the strange woman on the bus at the end of *Doomed Fruit*, Journey Prize Winner for 2006. (Or, in the case of fantasists, Lothlauriel, the treacherous elf queen who gets killed by bats in *Empire Resurgent: Book XII*.)

2. There are also moments when I look at my carefully saved mementoes and think, who are they for? I have scrapbooks full of newspaper clippings, and some of my stories are really quite good—worthy of being reread, I'd say. Like to look? I didn't think so.

3. And I wonder occasionally about my epitaph. I buried my mother's ashes under a birch tree with a verse from *Antony and Cleopatra*: "Age cannot wither her, nor custom stale / Her infinite variety." My ashes will probably end up in a planter after being bought at a garage sale as potting sand. My obituary will read: "Laurel Bernard, wife of John, cf. Dr. Oliver Sacks, *The Man Who Mistook His Wife for a Potting Mix*. Survived by no children and no grandchildren, but she did get the odd thank-you note from nieces and nephews. RIP [Rest in Planter]."

Suddenly, looking at this, being childless seems like a guarantee of oblivion. It occurs to me that in writing our parents' memorials, we may write our own, and Shakespeare's lines could mean either that Cleopatra was immortal or that she lived briefly, stuck to nothing and left no lasting achievement behind. But this, of course, is why I'm writing a book.

I really must finish it.

Laurel Bernard, who lives in Victoria, B.C., is an editor and writer currently alternating between writing articles, newspaper desk work, *Hansard* transcription and book editing. She is also writing a mystery novel about a psychic, a sidekick and a dog.

a small conclave
of chairs

RITA MOIR

MY FAVOURITE-EVER SYMPATHY CARD came from a kid at the Whole School next to where I live. Almost 10 years ago when my old dog died, I returned home to a bundle of handmade cards propped against my oval-glassed front door. The cards were made with construction paper heavily glued with sparkles and coloured feathers. My favourite, from Tash, was plastered with green and red glitter, since Christmas was in the offing.

In purple, gold and silver lettering, Tash wrote: "I'm so sorry Connor died. I know how much he meant to you. My dog got hit by a snowplow and died, my hamster got eaten by a cat and I was really sad for me too!" It's pretty hard to top that for tragedy, and Tash gave me a great laugh.

I'm caretaker for the Vallican Whole Community Centre, a 35-year-old institution that is home to the school where Tash was a student. The Vallican Whole sits between the mountains and the Little Slocan River, which flows into the Slocan. Set in a cedar-hemlock forest, with huge windows letting in the sun, the community hall is a great place for a school. Out in the bush, you see forts and bike jumps, little conclaves of chairs, as if the kids hold the same kind of endless meetings their parents have held for years. I live in my log home next door, a stone's throw from the building. I've lived in the Kootenays of British Columbia for 30 years, since we arrived from Alberta to build the caretaker's house; I've lived here since I was 23, when I was old enough to have babies but didn't. In those early years, as we built the hall and the school settled in, I knew each child, the child's parents and relatives, their dogs and hamsters.

Now I know few of the kids. They come, they grow up, they're gone. I've become the witch next door who leans out her window and hollers over at them, in a kind but no-nonsense voice, much like my own mother's, "Get out of the flower garden!" The implied ending of "you little morons" goes unsaid. I'm not heartless: at the sound of a child's cry, I'm down the ladder from my tower and out my back door in a flash. If they bleed, I will bandage. If they cry, I will console.

But I am not a mother. Never have been. I was a stepmother for three years. For a year here, or a year there, I have taken in kids whose own families couldn't cope. They stayed in the spare room, next to my own, close to the school, secure in my care. But no, I am not a mother.

⚷ My own mother was the best. My sisters are both mothers. But my brothers are not fathers, and though it's the first time I've thought of it this way, I am the girl in the family who made the same choice as the boys. There is an indelible scene from our childhood. Dad is building our house, a structure that will stand for the rest of our lifetime as our family home, a testament to his skills. He drives a nail into an interior door frame. He and my mother have words in one of those rarely witnessed, intimate moments of parental strain.

"You hammer a nail and it lasts forever," she says. "I wash the dishes and three hours later I wash the same damned dishes again."

I'm with you on that one, Mum. And I'm with you, too, Dad. I'm gonna hammer nails. I'm never gonna be stuck washing anyone's dishes. A pile of dirty, or even clean dishes, will never be my cairn.

There's something I still grapple with: when I was 17, in 1969, my mother left us. She abandoned what was becoming the Stepford Wives' life of a faculty wife in Brandon, Manitoba; she walked out so she could claim her own training and career. It was a wrenching decision she made, to leave several of us teenagers at home, later to send for my younger sister after she got settled, and head to Minnesota.

Our ranch-style house, its large picture window facing a cul-de-sac, seemed empty without her laughter, her steam. I didn't know if she was leaving for a while or forever, but I got it completely and I cheered her on. It was plain that she was dying inside, that with much more of Brandon, or at least the life she led in Brandon, her soul would be sucked clean away. I have no recollection of the day she left. In those heady days of intellectual and political ferment in the 1960s, the days of Betty Friedan and *The Feminine Mystique*, all change was possible and necessary. You go, Mum, I would have said, had there been such a parallel expression for mothers as there is now for their girl children.

It was not a logical contradiction, despite the feminist revolution just underway and my own burgeoning feminism, that I became the surrogate mother to my older brothers and younger sister. Someone had to hold the fort while Mum was gone. Dad worked long days at the university, and I'm not certain what ruse he invented to cover Mum's move. She was away training for a job, I expect. Meanwhile, we had to keep the home front operating. It was hard, it ground me down, but I was proud, too. I held up my portion of that cold prairie sky—I overachieved at school and in sports; I smashed my frustration out on field-hockey balls and the shins of my opponents. I played hard, too, partied hard and had lots of friends. And I saw exactly what being a mother meant.

It was difficult for all of us, but damn it, our mother had mothered us and all our friends. She'd mothered our community: when we held protest marches against the Vietnam War in Brandon's little Stanley Park (oh, how we loved it that we had our own Stanley Park: not everything happened in Vancouver!), we could bring home the whole demonstration of 30 people, and she'd feed us hot stew. We'd bring home rebellious military brats from the nearby base in Shiloh; we'd bring home the beaded, the longhaired, the halt and lame. When there were kids who needed "taking in," as we called it back then, she took them in. She'd given to us as a nuclear family and to the greater "us," an extended family, and I wanted to give back. I wanted my mother to succeed out in the world, so when she left, I tried to be her and do what she did on a daily basis.

I ironed; I baked oatmeal cookies, brownies and date squares. I saw them get eaten and I baked again. Then I washed the cookie sheets and cleaned the house as my dad went to work, my brothers held down part-time jobs and went to school. Our house became a haven for draft resisters up from the States, and my young sister and father fought their ferocious battles unrefereed by my mother. Our family became a loose-knit bunch of people living in the same home, as strangers came and went. I saw what my mother had done, over and over and over again to make us a family; without her, we struggled. We all worked hard to make a go of it and we survived, but I remember clearly that I took on the main job of mothering. She needed our support, and for the love of Christ, she wasn't going to hear a bunch of shit from home about how it was too hard for all of us.

Living part of her life was a valuable lesson. Mum fought with her guilt about leaving, and still does, but she did it and held out for changes: some accommodation from my father, which he made. She demanded that for once in his life, he follow where she led. When he did that, our family was together again. She showed me bargaining tools about domestic life: that you can negotiate and even go out on strike.

But the big lesson for me was that kids, and there were five of us, take everything. After my taste of young motherhood, I was never willing to give everything away again.

⚮ I heard the biological clock tick once, in a gooey romantic moment in the Ainsworth hot springs, floating in the amniotic fluid of early love, the steam rising from the water as snow shone on the mountains: Should we make babies, my partner and I googooed, bobbling close and sliding against each other: Ooh, aah. Then my brain kicked in: No, it said. And I listened.

There were other logical reasons, of course, or at least reasons that seemed logical in our young political, analytical minds, with each partner I've had. My first had a father so threatening and institution-alized that he feared he'd repeat the pattern. So we did all the things to our nubile, fertile bodies that you have to do to stop pregnancies: Dalkon Shield, pills, foam, gloppy round things that spring out and shoot across the room or, successfully inserted, are later removed. Finally, vasectomy.

And now? After several long-term relationships and no children, there's menopause. No more birth control. No more decisions. Full stop.

⚮ I am maternal, but I'm not a mother. And therefore, somewhat to my bewilderment, because I am an intelligent person, I understand the biological sequitur: no children, ergo, no grandchildren. Of course I've seen the women, a few generations older than me, in my immediate community, become grandmothers, then great-grandmothers. Women like T.C. Carpendale who, at age 53 when we moved here three de-cades ago, became a kind of surrogate mother to most of the young hippie community. But still, her life and offspring were just part of the huge mix of all of us roaring around building our lives. T.C. and her brood were building homes, building the hall, and during this frenzy, she, like a quarterback, carried the ball of motherliness and grand-motherliness for the rest of us.

But the issue of grandmotherhood gobsmacks me now when my contemporaries, my feminist friends, the ones I grew up with around here and with whom I made the revolution—fighting the pro-choice and health-care battles, for midwifery and decent job training and equal pay, and making our culture and community halls and singing in choirs and building housing for seniors and engaging in struggles over water and forests (and trust me, we're not against logging, my best friends and I)—my feminist friends who are now more settled, these feminist revolutionaries ask, "Oh, have I shown you the latest?" And they open their little brag books, their faces aglow as they show me the picture of Enzo or Leona, or Dawson and Sydney and Madeleine.

I look at the babies; I look even more to my friends' faces, and my heart bursts for them. A little voice inside me says, "Yikes!" I don't believe I've seen my friends happier. As if the cares, the struggles, the years of taking the hard stands in the community, melt from their skin. The lines are gone, their cheeks are creamy and their eyes shine with love and pride. They are completed and connected; they are of and with their children and family once more in a new, rich way.

The big "Oops!" blooper bubbles from my frontal lobe. As if the message, "You'll regret it if you don't have babies," is finally getting its laugh track. My friends haven't given up their political or community life. They are active and engaged. The new babies haven't turned them into mush. But they are absorbed and enlarged in some way that will never be mine, because I never made the same choices and sacrifices they made to become mothers.

The sacrifices and the joys involve courage I can only witness and imagine. My older sister Judy's younger son died in a plane crash just a few years ago. William's death is becoming the heart of our lives, not in a morbid way but in how you survive the worst you can imagine. How could I write about motherhood without talking about my sister Donna, who stands by her daughters through the hardest times: Maggie, 16, one minute fine, bright and lively, and the next in the emergency ward, stricken with fibromyalgia; Erin, just 22, fights with drugs and street life and institutionalization. I hold my life next to my sisters' and feel both regret and relief that I have never had to be as strong as them. I try to be a good sister, but there are days I know I could have contributed more. I could have borne children to carry on our family, to contribute the kind of laughter and strength that only children can give.

$\wp$ I know that by being nobody's mother, I've reaped advantages that most mothers couldn't. I've packed my car and notebooks and taken off to live and work across Canada. I've settled into mining towns and fishing villages. I've worked in political campaigns and legislative offices, CBC studios, factories and restaurants. I've holed up in little motel rooms, met strangers who've become lifetime friends. I've worked strange, long hours without upsetting anyone else. I've fallen in love across the country without, by those instabilities, hurting any children.

But now I see my friends with their grandbabies and acknowledge that I am jealous, one step removed. Perhaps the wanderlust is over, and now I envy these women I love and the reinvigoration of their families. These women are my community; their children were the children of my community. Inevitably, these kids moved away and made their lives, and now, like the ducks that arrive each spring to raise their broods, they're returning to raise their children. I see them in the grocery store parking lot, or at a demonstration to support the teachers. It is wonderful to run into them, but I am isolated from them by the simple fact that I don't have children. I am not part of a multiplying, reproductive clan. And so, the disconnect grows greater because their world is work and children and family. It is, increasingly, the world of their mothers, my closest friends, too.

I'm not sure I get it, yet. I could, and probably will, just pick up the phone and say, include me. Come over, all of you. What can I do? Can I babysit? But I have to sit with this first, nurse this new phenomenon. Politically and intellectually, I never bought the line I heard as a young woman: that in my old age I would regret having no one to care for me. Phooey. Lots of old people have kids who don't care for them. I could name you six. I always figured I'd rather work on building a social community that took care of its old people than rely on my own private investment. But still…

It's easy to get isolated. Anyone can, whether you live close to neighbours in the city, or far down snowed-in winter roads in the country. I am becoming isolated from young people, really young people, even though I am surrounded by them. The little kids at the school come and go; they shriek and grab long sticks from my woodpile. Some I like and can horse around with, sit down and talk with. Others I could cheerfully throttle. I hope they all go live happy and productive lives. But I don't really know them.

This is the weird part about being childless and living far from your own blood kin: you end up without that organic connection to youth and regeneration. When there is death and mourning, there's no little kid in your living room giving you that "life goes on" feeling. There's no family group snuggling around the hearth.

Hmm. The issue was never that I wouldn't have a child to mop my spittle when I'm drooling porridge down my chin. It's that I won't light up at the little tykes simply carrying on with the business of living, and that someday my community of mothers, piddling alongside me in our Pampers for the post-ambulatory, will beam at that sweet line of life before them, and their pride and laughter lines will deepen in a way that mine never can. A person could get downright maudlin as the snow falls and we head into December. A little middle-aged angst to throw into the stewpot of a Canadian winter. That political button,

"Oops, I forgot to have kids," once seemed funny, but there are days now when its flippancy grates.

Well, I didn't, and that's that. You just have to keep taking stock and reassessing things, that's all. You make choices and live with the worst and best of them. Oddly (and now I do sound like an old bat), it takes a good funeral to jerk your angst-smitten brain around.

⚘ A month ago I attended the burial and memorial for T.C. Carpendale, the mother of us all I mentioned earlier. In fact, we used that reference so often at her memorial that her daughter even joked about it. The first thing you'd notice about T.C. was her shock of white hair and those piercing blue eyes you would never lie to. She has sisters who look like her; together they were an armada of small ancients. T.C. had arms that would embrace you; armed with her approval and her faith, you would go forth like a warrior. She died at 86. She had a good life. Her death was sad, but not tragic. She left a wealth of family and works to be proud of, including us, her community.

T.C.'s family carried her coffin up to the cemetery. We built the cemetery 25 years ago, when our community hall society (and of course T.C. was part of it) figured we'd better have a burial ground. It's a rural graveyard, in the forest, surrounding open grasses. T.C.'s grave now is the first one you see when you walk in. Her burial happened at the time of year when the larches are yellow and the air is cold with the whiff of snow.

T.C.'s son made her coffin. Her grandchildren and friends dug her grave. Her clan of 50 did all the work so that on that Friday afternoon, after they had recited their poetry and sung their songs, she could be lowered into the earth. They lifted the heavy sculpture of a pregnant woman, which her daughter made 20 years ago, onto the mound. The grandkids planted bulbs to come up in spring. The next day at our community hall, we filed in, family and friends. The floor we walked on, T.C. had sanded. The window frames, she had painted. We could look around and see her everywhere, in the memories of her dandelion and elderberry wine we'd auctioned at outrageous prices to raise funds for the hall. Speaker after speaker paid her tribute: she had supported who we were as we struggled in our new lives. Our young families looked like hers, and in this our lives were confirmed.

We weren't her children. But as I looked around, to the kids who are now in their 20s and 30s and 40s with their own kids, as I looked to my closest, heart-of-my-heart friends, now greying, as I listened to the best speakers and singers and poets a community can summon forth, I heard over and over how T.C., besides raising her brood of six, stood sentinel for hundreds of us, through all the screw-ups as we forged our young community, until we grew up enough to govern ourselves. She served on the boards of our community hall, the school, the seniors' housing society and the cemetery. In all of this, her presence and calm and humour were motherly gifts.

T.C. didn't have to be our mother to mother us. We didn't have to be her children to help lay her to rest.

That day in our hall, I saw the kids I came to know and love long ago, in the days when I knew their families, their dogs and their hamsters. They'd come to support T.C.'s family, and they'd come to celebrate a larger family, too: our small rural community. At that moment, it didn't matter if we, individually, had children or were childless. It didn't matter because we have become a large family to each other over the decades.

T.C. is a lesson against becoming maudlin. In this contemplation of childlessness, a person could become regretful. I could have looked around during her burial and later at her memorial and seen only her fine family of four generations. But I also saw a community.

My life is rich with family: my blood family who live far away in Manitoba and Minnesota and Nova Scotia; my family made here by our collective effort, my community where I live in the Slocan Valley. I don't think of myself as childless. I never really have. I simply didn't have children.

Rita Moir is a former journalist who now writes creative non-fiction in Vallican, B.C. Her most recent book is *The Windshift Line: A Father and Daughter's Story*, about her American-born father, a botanist. Her first book was *Survival Gear*; her next, *Buffalo Jump: A Woman's Travels*, won the 2000 Hubert Evans Non-Fiction Prize and the 2000 VanCity Book Prize. Her essay, "Leave Taking" won an *Event* creative non-fiction award in 1989 and has appeared in numerous anthologies.

autumn fruit

PATRICIA FRANK

MY BIRTH CANAL HAS NOT BIRTHED, my arms have not cradled a child and these breasts have not suckled. I am without progeny. How do I feel about that?

Pretty good.

Some smart psychotherapist or geneticist will have to explain why I was born without the urge to reproduce. When other women's biological clocks began ticking, my clock moved silently; in fact, so silently that it bore an "Out-of-Order" sign.

Throughout my life, and I now approach 60, I've wondered about that, wondered if lacking the reproductive urge made me somehow less of a woman, as though I were flawed and missing a vital component. After all, we live in a society that expects women to bear children and to find satisfaction as mothers and caretakers of *kinder*, hearth and crockpot. This supposed state of bliss flies in the face of all the Valium that mothers of my parents' generation ingested. The popular book of the day, *Valley of the Dolls*, recorded those pill-filled lives.

Today, oceans of Ambien soothe the women who have everything—kids, home, job, sometimes spouse—yet are still unsatisfied.

Poor woman, you must be depressed; here, swallow this pill. Still a valley of the dolls, except those now taking the dolls work full-time.

I found one explanation for my missing brood in astrology. More than one description of my Sun sign, Gemini, has said that Gemini is a "barren" sign and that those of us born under the sign of the Twins often do not bear children. Is it because we have two personas contained within? One, a logical, responsible adult and the other, a child of wonder, always questioning and seeking adventures? Are we Geminis parents of our own internal children? That wise bard/Gemini Walt Whitman understood this odd dichotomy when he said, "Do I contradict myself? ... I contain multitudes."

Is being a Gemini the answer, I ask? I tick off on my fingers all the Geminis I know who are not child-free and can think of only one, who birthed a son. Then she decided to spurn men altogether and has become a meditative recluse. But she's not really alone, is she? She contains multitudes.

If my unparenting state is not due to genetics, and not to astro-logical happenstance, then what? Perhaps it's a learned behaviour.

My mother was one of those reluctant moms who followed the crowd and birthed three children. Living in a small, satellite town 12 miles from Philadelphia, Mom was isolated—truly wed to her house. She stopped driving when she married. I'm not sure why.

Mom was not a happy housewife wearing a ruffled apron and high heels, merrily baking pies and frolicking about the house with a feather duster. No, she was rather a malcontent who would have preferred to work, but my dad wouldn't have it. Dad was one of those quaint, old-fashioned men (or controlling, chauvinistic authoritarian, your choice) who spoke from his power position: "No wife of mine's going to work. What would people think? That I can't support my family."

Note that nothing of my mother's needs entered the equation. So Mom stifled her intelligence and tried to find fulfillment in Brownie meetings and the PTA. She damped down her emotions with vast quantities of Valium, ironed while watching television soaps and suffered, I suspect, from low-level depression all her days.

All our basic needs were met. I don't mean to complain. We had meals and clean clothes, but Mom was not quite there in spirit. She only came alive when my dad, a professional salesman, won vacation trips for two to exotic locations. Then, how my mom's face would light up; she'd become another person altogether. I felt a sense of dismay and abandonment as she went, freshly coiffed and smiling, to the Bahamas or Mexico, and once to pre-Castro Cuba. How happy she seemed to leave us.

Later, when I saw photos of those trips, my mother, who was usually garbed in faded housedresses, appeared glamorous in cocktail dresses, dangling faux-diamond earrings, red, red lipstick. And smiling, oh yes, smiling. Laughing with head thrown back, mouth wide open. Did this affect my decision to be an unparent? I do not know. I do know that my mother was happiest without us. Far away from us.

Several years after Alan and I married, I broke the news to my mom, with some hesitation and nervousness. "Mom, I've got something to tell you ..."

"What is it?" she asked, a worried look on her face.

"Well, Mom, Alan and I have decided ..."

"You're not getting a divorce, are you?"

Divorce would be a family first. We didn't do divorces in my family. We took Valium instead.

"No, Mom, nothing like that, it's just that, we've decided ..."

"What is it, already?" Mom demanded. "What??"

"Well, Mom, Alan and I have talked it over, and we agree that ... well, we've decided not to have children."

There, I'd said it.

Mom looked at me with a strange expression. Then she smiled a small smile and said, "Good decision. Wish I hadn't."

I didn't know then, and I still don't know today, whether that comment was a statement of utter honesty or a remark made deliberately to hurt me. Did she mean she wished she hadn't had me, personally, or children in general? At the time, I was so taken aback that I left the room with eyes brimming. We never spoke of it again. And my mom never asked for grandchildren from me. She had four grandchildren already. Perhaps that was a sufficiency.

I find children interesting, in theory and in person, at certain ages. They are quite miraculous as newborns, all soft, dewy and fuzzy; disturbing and nerve-wracking at 2 or 3, the age of "no" and screams and tears; enchanting at 4 through 12, and much too loud and rawly emotional as teenagers. I never wanted to have one of my own. I'm glad to have them visit—and glad when they go home.

Children are so very full-time and all-consuming, aren't they?

That's why I admire mothers. I think most every mother deserves accolades, rewards, flowers, chocolate, spa days, foot massages and full-time household help. It takes courage, commitment and devotion to fulfill their 20-something-year parental contract. If Mom were around today, I'd tell her so. And I'd like to revisit that comment she made. It needs clarification. Instead, I walled it away in a solitary place, and it grew scar tissue. But those words wound me still.

Truth be told, I never quite forgave her. Her remark changed me and changed our relationship. That makes me sad, as I think she was a woman who needed love. Her own mother, my grandmother, had been tight-lipped and grim, quick to criticize, slow to compliment. She was an unhappy woman, with five children, a war-damaged husband and a grocery store to run. What dreams passed her by?

An idle comment from my mother, and my heart closed into a fist. I felt like a mistake, a choice made for convention and not from love. I was born nine months after the end of the Second World War. I imagine that I was made during a night of exuberant celebration. War's end, the end of rationing. I could have been butter.

Once, I gathered my courage and ended a mother-daughter phone conversation with "I love you, Mom," and met silence from the other end. Shall we call it a pregnant pause or, in my case, a very long unpregnant pause, filled with hope? But "I love you, too" was not forthcoming.

In a way, Mom's indifference was freeing. I felt the apron strings untying. Time to leave the needy child behind. Alan and I headed west and didn't stop until we hit the rugged coast of northern California. There we found, in the early 1970s, a paradise for those who had open minds and spirits. I took strength from the redwoods and found comfort in the hills, where I hiked for miles. Everything seemed possible in those heady days—except having children. We were a family unto ourselves.

Dutiful daughter still, I sent the Mother's Day cards and occasional flower arrangements across the continent, but I never felt the same toward her. Part of me gave up and sought validation and support from husband and friends, and from myself, the most challenging person of all.

Has it been an unfortunate decision? Do I have regrets or second thoughts now that I am past child-bearing years? I've searched my heart to respond in honesty and I must say, with a bit of Edith Piaf's Parisian accent, "No, no regrets."

Whether being no one's mother came from genetic design, a plane-tary and solar fluke or familial imprinting, I do not know. Reasons do not matter; the fact remains: I have chosen not to recreate another being. And it's okay. More than okay, for much pleasure's been mine. More arrives daily. True, there have been times of dark despair, self-doubt and crushed hope. Times when my Trickster mind asks, "What might I have become if she'd loved me more, encouraged me?" But those moments ebb, fade.

Anger has worn away, watered by old tears.

My life is full, and I know moments of great joy. A beloved and loving husband and dear, wise friends are warmly knit into the fabric that is my life. And nature, always nature, is there to comfort and teach me.

I have walked ridgetop trails in the yellow hills of California and met a mountain lion. I've swum with turquoise and gold tropical fish in the shadow of Mayan ruins in Mexico's Yucatan. And once, for a fleeting second, touched a dolphin in Hawaii's sea.

And today? Like the salmon, I've returned to my native waters—but not to spawn. We've moved back to the east coast and now dwell in a tiny coastal hamlet in North Carolina. I follow sandpipers on the beach.

The words Anne Morrow Lindbergh wrote in *Gift from the Sea* keep me company: "One is forced against one's mind, against all tidy resolutions, back into the primeval rhythms of the seashore." I've found sand wears away the hard places—on feet and heart. Peace descends. Mother Ocean brings me home. Wisdom comes slowly, but it comes.

The passage of years, considerable reflection, many self-help books and a spot of therapy have all helped me to like the wonder-kid within. I know now I was given as much love as my mother was capable of giving. And if not loved with a conventional, Hallmark-greeting-card love, I have learned how to mother myself.

I cuddle the interior child, give her lots of encouragement. She's a nice kid, a bit tender and shy, but then, she had a rocky beginning. I expect she's going to shine. A late bloomer, true, but fall flowers can be so brilliant when they bloom before winter. I think of myself as a golden mum, aglow, pregnant with potential.

Patricia Frank does freelance writing for national magazines and newspapers from her home in the coastal hamlet of Beaufort, North Carolina—where Rachel Carson lived and wrote for a while. After 32 years in Oakland and San Francisco, she has stopped her roving—for now. The dolphins have secrets to share. The tides bring peace. Between assignments, she's writing on the topic of women and nature and trying to perfect the flow of her sun salutation.

patchwork

MARY JANE COPPS

AT 47, I AM A WOMAN WHO MAKES DECISIONS — and acts on them. I'm teased about it, told I should have a business card that reads, "Mary Jane — She Gets Things Done." There is joy for me in the doing, in helping others do, achieve, grow.

But the decision not to have children — I never made that decision. Well, I did, but then I changed my mind and then I changed it again and then … I am not childless by choice, although many of my choices have contributed to my being childless. I live with this as regret and blessing both, a point of chaos within my ordered life.

My boyfriend and I are deep in conversation about the future.

"When we get married," I say, "I won't be changing my name."

Marriage is a comfortable subject between us. Love at 18 includes forever. He doesn't take me seriously. I remain adamant. He becomes annoyed, even frightened.

"If it's so important we have the same name," I challenge, "then you change yours."

This revolutionary notion silences him. We never speak of it again.

My clarity did not come from a feminist awakening. In my small-town Catholic world, I hadn't even heard the word yet, let alone understood the philosophy. No, my impassioned stance came from a gestating belief: I could protect myself from my parents' legacy, distance myself from my likeness to my mother, by simply doing the opposite.

And for more than a decade, I would live and love based on this belief. I would keep my own name, have my own bank account, never wear a girdle, smoke, shun diamonds, silverware and china, and cease to consider having babies an essential part of life.

Opposite was my talisman, a necessary magic to vanquish the power of the past, the influence of blood ties.

Natasha is my oldest stepdaughter. We meet when she is 11 and I am 23. She is annoyed at sharing her father's brief visit with me, terrified of losing her dad. We stumble through that first day of ice cream, movies and pizza, and somehow she decides knowing me is okay.

With me, she purchases her first pair of high heels, lives both within and without my marriage to her father, celebrates her jazz performance at New York's Birdland and walks down the aisle at her wedding. While I struggle with this essay, she calls to say she's pregnant, asks me to be in the delivery room.

Natasha ceaselessly worries about disappointing those she loves, losing them. "Tash," I say, "there is nothing you can do that could make me stop loving you. Nothing." This is unconditional. This is parent and child.

Since I was the youngest child, September robbed me of my sibling playmates, left me to entertain myself. Sometimes I would rifle through the "adult" cupboards looking for treasure, like the black and gold boxes of baby clothes. I loved them. Awed by their tiny perfection, I would pile them on my bed, tie and snap them into place around dolls that floated inside. Then Santa delivered a life-sized baby doll I christened Noreen, after a favoured cousin. She could wear all the baby clothes. I helped her stiff limbs into jackets, nighties and noisy plastic pants, tied bonnets snugly under her chin.

But I knew that good mothers needed more than just clothes for a baby, and my mother soon delivered the necessary item—a white and silver baby carriage with a blue vinyl hood on accordion hinges. In seconds, Noreen and I were out the door, endlessly walking up and down the one block of sidewalk outside my house.

It isn't that I didn't do other things. I wore my brothers' hand-me-downs, climbed trees, played army in the bush, caught salamanders and toads in coffee tins. But boys my age also played house, and every house had a baby. I did not doubt, did not question, that boys became husbands and fathers, that I would become a wife and mother to many, many babies.

❧ Nina stomps to the car behind her sister, joy and anger playing across her face. She is eight years old, her father is her hero and she has absolutely no interest in me.

My exotic stepdaughter creates beauty, captures inner visions in pottery, photography. And she is fierce—independent, stubborn. We have this in common; it becomes the foil we fence with, each of us inflicting near-fatal blows more than once.

After two years of almost-silence, we share the tasks of a family wedding. We apologize, squirm in our seats. She looks down at her hands and says, "People ask me, you know, where I get it from, my discipline, my focus. They ask if I get it from my mom, or my dad. And I tell them it's neither. I tell them I get it from you." We, too, are parent and child.

❧ Nothing is right. Christmas makes that obvious. My two brothers, drunk, battle the tree, let it fall to the floor twice before lassooing it with a drapery cord and tying it lopsidedly in place. Disgusted, I leave, go out into a skin-numbing, snow-squeaking, minus-40-degree night, walk for hours trying to evade a heavy loneliness. At 17, I have buried both parents, my dad just six weeks ago.

Nothing is right.

In January, my oldest brother says the unthinkable—there's no money. Dad left no will. In time it will all work out, but for now I have to get a job. Exams are in three weeks; I'm vice-president of the student council. A job? He's got it all figured out: a waitress friend needs a babysitter for her three-year-old. I can go there from school, child asleep after dinner, plenty of time for studying, home by midnight.

Okay.

Our groceries consist of cheap cuts of meat and blocks of bright orange cheese. I'm up at 6:00 A.M., setting timers, adding onions and potatoes to the grey slabs that will be the evening's dinner.

Every day I rush from school to the apartment and the little blond girl who does not yet speak in words. No one has read to her. No one has talked to her. Noon is when her day starts, with a nap, before I arrive. She stays awake until her mother comes home, accompanied always by a man, never the same man. They all offer me a lift in their cars, but I say no, pretend to call a cab, but hold tight to the money and walk home in the dark.

Nothing is right.

In February, the mother and I speak quickly in the doorway as she rushes to work. I bang snow from my boots, call to the little girl. She does not run toward me. She stands at the dryer, stringing together her nonsense sounds, poking a mouth-dampened finger at each button. I squat beside her, arms open, but she windmill-slaps away my hug, pushes me. The dryer is today's toy of choice.

A peculiar, faraway sound. What have you put in the dryer? "No," she screams. "No." Just a minute, sweetie, I'm only going to check.

Click goes the button. Pop goes the door. Inside, a tiny white kitten. Has it already been tumbled? How did this happen? Who's loving this child? Who's loving this kitten? Who's loving me?

There is a sound in my head, waves crashing to shore. I release the kitten, and it runs to an unreachable corner. I take the screaming child in my arms, absorb her kicks and punches. I too am crying, in shudders, in gasps. They have no end. The little girl falls silent in this storm, recovers a doll from the floor, jabbers away quietly. I shiver and weep. Nothing stops the tears. Three phone calls and I find my brother. Now, you must come now.

At home, I go upstairs, leave my brother to deal with the little girl and her mother. I bury myself between sheets, wanting to be that kitten—unreachable, untouchable, invisible. The storm rages within me. I break.

At nine, I read constantly, choose to sit in the back seat of the car, with a pile of books, travelling in chapters instead of miles.

"They seem lovely," my mom says, talking to my dad about the new young couple on our block.

"Yes," my dad says. "We should invite them over soon."

"But it's very sad, don't you think? Their not having any children. They aren't that young. She must be barren."

This is a Bible word I don't understand, so I ask.

"That she can't have babies," my mother says. "That God has made her unable to get pregnant."

"Maybe they just don't want to have children," I say, shrugging off the conversation, wanting to get back to my book.

"That would be a sin," says my dad.

"Yes," says my mom. "You get married to have babies. To be married and not have children is to go against God."

"Oh," I say.

Ɛ Angel Johnson came into my life when I was 36, or rather I came into hers, as a volunteer at the Boys and Girls Club in Toronto's Regent Park. She is athletic, artistic and brilliant. She is sarcastic, skeptical and tough. During our first three months of weekly homework sessions she almost scared me away—almost. When she turned 10, our relationship evolved to include her grandmother, her teachers and weekend activities.

In those days, Angel did not believe in promises. Her experience was that "later" meant "never." The phrase "Can I have?" was an incessant part of our time together. Finally I took a stand.

"Angel," I said, stopping in the middle of a sidewalk. "Tell me, have I ever made a promise I haven't kept?"

Fifteen feet in front of me, she looked back quizzically, then focused on her shoes, deep in thought.

"No," she said, looking up, surprised.

"Have I given you any reason to believe that I'm going to start breaking promises?"

"No."

"Right. Can you stop begging now? Can you believe that I will always do my best to keep my word? Please?"

"Yes," she said. "Yes, I can do that."

She did. She still does.

Ɛ When I am 16, my dad and I spend an hour on Thursday nights watching television. I make Pillsbury turnovers just before 9:00 P.M., and we settle in the den to watch *Kojak*.

I develop a bit of a crush on Telly Savalas, who plays the tough but big-hearted city detective. I take to reading movie magazines in the grocery store. I am shocked to discover that his grandmother gave birth to more than 20 children.

I didn't even know it was possible for a woman to be pregnant— always. I fall in love with the idea, desire for myself a big, endless family.

❧ I arrive at the hospital with file folders and a smoked-meat sandwich from the deli near our office. My business partner is bed-bound. Her water has broken at 30 weeks; she's on constant fluids; her husband is encouraged to go back to work; the nurses have asked her to find tasks to keep her occupied.

While we talk, she leans over, makes tiny marks on a piece of paper. "What are you doing?" I ask.

"Recording contractions," she says. "They've been false alarms, but I like to keep track."

She is ticking too often for my liking. I wave at a nurse, who investigates and announces, "Five centimetres," while shifting the bed to make room for a gurney.

I dial and dial for her husband, but can't find him. I leave messages, race to the doorway as the gurney rolls down the hall.

"Do you want me to come with you?"

"Yes," is the anxious reply.

So at 33 I'm in the delivery room, with her husband, when Owen is born, red and annoyed. And when he is one, we begin a ritual that lasts until he is 12, spending time together once a week. When he is about four, I hug him and say, "I love you."

"Mary Jane," he says. "I know you love me. You don't have to say it any more."

❧ My life is great; my life is a disaster. I spend my energy living on a tightrope.

I am 28. Edward and I have been together for five years, and we are thrashing about in the dregs of our relationship. When his father died suddenly, four years earlier, our sexual relationship vanished. We have affection, laughter, friendship—which only confuses me. I am both ignorant and naive; too embarrassed to seek counsel and too in love to acknowledge the facts. Hope propels me forward. Fear traps me in silence.

There are exciting diversions. I now carry my briefcase to the corner of Bay and College in Toronto, to work for Canada's largest magazine publisher. And we've replaced our renovated east-end semi with a three-storey Victorian in Kensington Market, a multicultural neighbourhood. With our upstairs tenants, we become a community that enjoys great food, abundant alcohol and parties that end when the cops show up.

One day, I come home exhilarated by my accomplishments at work. Edward and a tenant are deep in philosophical discussion; the living-room table holds bottles of imported beer. I join them, itching with excitement. We interrupt ourselves long enough to decide on Chinese food, a walk to Spadina. On the way home, we stop at our corner Portuguese bar, sit outside with more beer, listen to snatches of Billy Idol performing at the Canadian National Exhibition.

Back in our living room, Edward pulls out a liqueur from Scotland, pours three glasses. I swallow mine in one sweet gulp, ask for more. The request is met with astonishment. My relationship with alcohol is, at best, cautious.

"Are you sure?" Edward asks.

"Yes, of course. I'm not even a bit drunk."

But within 30 minutes, I am drunk beyond my means, beyond memory. Edward stays up all night, holding my head, my hand, grateful to escape for work in the morning. I face myself in the bathroom mirror, struggle with an unknown body pain and tremendous guilt.

At dinner I am full of apologies, can't believe I allowed such a thing to happen. Edward shakes it off; he's lived through many hangovers of his own.

"But I can't remember anything," I say.

"That's probably good," he says. "Every time I thought you were finally asleep, you'd suddenly sit up in bed screaming: 'I'm my mother. I'm my mother.' "

℘ Owen's sister, Isobel, arrives in 1995. She is born wise. I can see it in her eyes. Athletic and agile, she always wants to show me what she can do: climbing my banister; a quick Highland fling in my kitchen; a few rows of very fine knitting. Whatever it is, she calls out to me, my name a tapestry of parent and friend: "MommaDaddyMaryJane?"

℘ Looking after other people's children, whether it is for March break or Friday lunch, brings with it a level of anxiety that must differ from what you feel when those children are your own. In my care, all the children have faded from sight inside busy stores. They have taken ill, their fever sending me dashing to the telephone. They have fallen, cut themselves, cried in pain for a wide variety of reasons I was sure their mother would understand instantly, but which caused me to fear the worst. And they have known me to command "Not on my watch," when I thought they were getting too close to an accident.

But none of this qualifies me to speak in a room full of mothers. Many times I have forgotten, spoken up when there's been a discussion about homework or discipline or illness.

"Do you have children?" someone will ask.

"Stepchildren," I say. "Godchildren."

"Oh," they say, and turn their faces inward, toward the circle of real mothers.

℘ "Nanny" is what her mother hopes she will call me, but my granddaughter may create a different word when the time comes. Whatever it is, I'll accept. In those astonished seconds of her arrival, as I watched her head and shoulders slide into our world, saw her parents' faces transformed by love, I did know regret. It was brief, a wish really, to have experienced childbirth, to have been the mother whose new baby settles on her breast. It vanished with the wonder of holding Naja Summer Helmer and knowing that, regardless of my choices, I have a big, endless family.

⚲ It is marriage, or rather the implosion of a marriage, that plunges me into my darkest panic. I cannot believe that love is not enough, cannot face myself, my failure, my future. I'm 35 and frantic to find light.

My search takes me to the office of a psychologist whose wisdom and care are life-giving, life-altering. She allows for my insistence that we focus only on me, not Edward, not my family, just me and how I have brought myself to this heart-shattering moment.

"Are you sure you don't want to investigate things involving your parents?" she asks.

"No, there's no need," I say. "I've dealt with all that."

How utterly foolish, but human, to want to move forward, not look too closely at the past. So we work together, week after week, uncovering behaviours and habits that make intimate relationships a struggle.

Finally, armed with several inspiring self-revelations, I tell the psychologist it's time for me to move on.

She hugs me goodbye and says, "Don't hesitate to call me if you think I can help."

Just over a year later I do call, do need help.

"It's about a decision I can't seem to make," I say. "And that's not like me. I'm sure it's just one appointment. If I made a list with you, of pros and cons, I'm sure it'll all become clear."

The decision is whether or not to become a single parent. I'm officially divorced, and firm in my stand that another marriage isn't in my future. I have the support of friends and family. One moment I'll be sure that having a baby is exactly the right thing to do. Within the hour, I'm sure it's the worst possible decision.

But lists don't help. There is an unnameable something, a fear, a terror. How do we find it?

"We go back," says the psychologist. "We go back to the beginning."

So we do. We find me at nine years of age, just outside Montreal on a small concrete island in the midst of oncoming traffic. Panicked by the dark and the speed of the cars, my mother has broken apart, forced my father to let her out, insisted that she take her "baby."

We revisit my first memory, a night in the kitchen when I am three and my mother, stoned and drunk, insists that as part of a game of "prove that you love me" each child must move a hand toward a fiery orange element until she says "stop."

And we find me as an infant, quiet and still inside my crib. Every sibling is at school. Dad is at work. Mom drinks down drugs with gin, passes out. Disturbing her brings a monster to my bedside, someone who looks like my mother but whose face is swollen and red, who screams at me to stop crying, to stop messing my diaper, to leave her alone. I do not want to rouse the monster. I stop crying. I ignore my kidneys and bowels. I am never hungry. I sit in my crib and wait quietly for my sister to come home from school.

There it is, the underlying navigator of my life. I do not want to rouse the monster—the me-myself-mother monster. There is no baby because I am afraid, have always been afraid, of being my mother.

But I am not my mother. I finally believe it. On the threshold of 40, it's okay, there can still be a baby. Slim chance, but a possibility.

Wait. Something's wrong. I'm not menstruating. Too much stress, that must be it. Moving from Toronto to Halifax, adjusting to so much change. I let another month go by. Nothing. I call the doctor. Nervous now. Could it be cancer? Some kind of serious infection?

No.

What then? What's wrong?

Nothing's wrong. You're fully menopausal. Very early. This kind of thing is genetic, runs in families. When did your mother start menopause?

I am not my mother.

Mary Jane Copps was born and raised in Timmins, Ontario, but now lives in Halifax, Nova Scotia. Her journalism appears in many places, and her fiction has been published in *The New Quarterly* and *A Room at the Heart of Things*, edited by Elizabeth Harvor. Her essay "In My Mother's Arms" appeared in *Dropped Threads 2*, edited by Carol Shields and Marjorie Anderson.

an oddity
in my culture

SADHNA DATTA

I AM A SINGLE WOMAN IN MY MID-40S, of East Indian origin. I do not have any children and I come from a fairly large family.

So how did I "escape" my destiny? Well, having a broad-minded mother helped, as did being the youngest of six children. I think my mother was just too tired to argue with me when it became my turn to get married. Marriage, and then having children, is a natural course of events for most societies. Indian families celebrate marriages and births of children with a great deal of ceremony.

Being the one who escaped all of that puts me somewhat on the periphery: Indian culture doesn't exactly have a place for me. I'm an oddity. Although I do know many women in my age group who are single and without children, the trend in recent years has been for the younger generations to get married at a younger age and start families almost immediately.

The mathematics is simple: since having children is a part of being married in the Indian culture, not being married automatically results in childlessness. In many North American families, being a mother outside the bounds of marriage, while not overtly sanctioned, is more readily accepted. In my culture, a woman who has children but is not married would stand out, perhaps bring her family disgrace.

I was fortunate enough to have two older sisters who went through the whole gamut of the "arranged marriage" and now both have children. I was 15 when my eldest sister, her marriage not working, left her husband and moved in with my mother. My sister was pregnant when she came to live with us. My mother, my twin brother and I became her family. When my nephew was born, although my mother was the main caregiver after my sister, I too had a role in raising him.

Being a "surrogate" mom definitely left an impression on me. I realized that raising a child as a single mother was hard work and emotionally taxing; it was not something I wanted to do.

It took a few years for my ideas to formulate. I became interested in the feminist movement during the late 1970s and started seeing women's roles from different angles. I began to regard marriage as a means of shaping women as "kept" beings, and I started to examine the role of motherhood. In my early 20s, I volunteered for an Indo-Canadian organization called India Mahila Association (IMA). We did outreach work for women of South Asian origin who were in dangerous situations or were fleeing abusive mates. Often these men would be violent toward their children as well. This got me thinking about the ties women have with their children—and often I noted a lack of similar connection between men and their offspring.

I remember feeling very angry toward the men and simultaneously wondering how society would view women who were as cruel to their children. We all know that society is judgmental about women considered to be bad or uncaring mothers. I kept pondering one question: "Is the main role for women, in world society, to be mothers?" I also wondered: "Why are men, to a certain degree, excluded from that responsibility? Shouldn't being a parent be viewed as equally important, regardless of gender?"

Armed with such questions, I made the decision not to have children. Since I had managed to sidestep the arranged-marriage issue, I was not sure I would get married at all. My work with IMA had also shown me that being married or just being with a partner was no guarantee that he would stick around to help me raise a child. Before I was 30, I had come to the conclusion that not only did society view the raising of children as a mother's job, but that in fact it was mostly women who were raising children. Whether these women were mired in abusive relationships or hired as top-notch executives of companies, motherhood was still regarded as their foremost role.

I've come to believe this is the situation in our society because I see such views reflected on a daily basis: in the media, reporting so many cases of actresses wanting desperately to save their marriages by having children; in two of my close friends and my eldest niece, feeling pressured to become mothers. My friends both decided to have children, and it changed their lives drastically. My niece is still thinking about it, but I fear family pressure will determine her decision.

All my siblings have children. In my family, I am The Aunt. (The Punjabi word is *masi*.) Even though I have played a significant role in the lives of my nieces and nephews, I am only that, an aunt. I don't think that my siblings have made any judgments about my decision to remain childless, but I do believe they view my role within our family as different from theirs. Since I do not have children to occupy me, they think I have more time on my hands than they do. Over the years I have been expected to shoulder certain family chores because I didn't have the added responsibilities of child-rearing. When my mother was alive, I was expected to spend a great deal of time with her. She called upon me to help with her banking or doctors' appointments. I usually assisted my eldest nephew (the one I helped my sister raise) to carry out these tasks. My mother's dependence on me as she aged also increased because I remained single.

In many ways, the roles between my mother and me were reversed as the years progressed: she became my child. When we argued, she would make offhand comments about how good it was that I didn't have any children. And I would reply, "Well, I have you, don't I?" When she passed away, I felt lost. I couldn't define my purpose in life. I'm sure mothers feel this way when they experience the empty-nest syndrome.

In Indian culture, if you don't have a husband and children, then the question that arises is, "What do you occupy your time with?" Though my immediate family has been supportive of my decision to remain childless, and my mother approved, the Indian community at large is less accepting: I'm an oddity. My mother perhaps made it easier for me because she moved from my place of birth in Nairobi, Kenya, where I would have been surrounded by more traditional relatives, to London, England, thus insulating me from the most critical "fallout."

Yet I do I feel as though I have often been judged as something of a nonentity by members of my larger community, due to my single, childless state. Even today, when an Indo-Canadian woman is not married by a certain age, it's suspected that something is "wrong" with her. She's likely to be pitied both because she is single and because she is childless. I find this attitude archaic—especially when applied to the many 40-something Indian women I know who lead vibrant, full lives. These women are contributing members of society; they own homes, run their own businesses, have professions, pay taxes and manage their own households. Nevertheless, they are viewed as incomplete, as though they have missed out on an important part of their lives. And when I meet someone I haven't seen for a while, the two questions I am most often asked are "So, you still haven't married?" and "Don't you miss having children?"

I regard parenting as an important role in society. However, I continue to ask, "Is it viewed in the same way for men? When men choose to remain single and childless, does society consider them incomplete?"

ς Choosing to remain childless is a decision I did not make lightly. I considered many factors. What if my mate did want children? What would my life be like as an elderly woman? Who would look after me? My eldest nephew is like a son to me. When I talk about these worries with him, his reply to me is always, "Well, of course I will look after you, Masi." It warms my heart to hear him say that he will take care of both my sister and me.

Deep within my soul I don't feel I've lost out on a wonderful experience. I have over the years been available and energetic enough to provide respite care for my sisters and brother by taking their children off their hands for a day or two. If I'd had children of my own, I might not have done that. I cherish the times I've had with all my nieces and nephews. However, when it comes time for them to go home to their parents, I'm relieved to have my own life back. I view myself as lucky, because taking care of children is not an easy job. Each time I do it, I'm reminded once again what an enormous undertaking it is to raise a family.

ς I don't know if my decision to become a teacher was in any way based on remaining childless. I don't think so, because I have early childhood memories of wanting to be a teacher. However, teaching only confirms that parenting is the hardest job on Earth.

I know I was lucky to be around my sister as she struggled to raise her son. Her experience had a huge impact on me. As he was growing up, my nephew quite often called me "Mom." And today, especially when they are engrossed in an activity or are distracted, my students sometimes also refer to me as "Grandma," "Grandpa," or "Mom." I like to hear that; it makes me feel a part of their lives.

When I've had to defend my decision not to have children, people respond, "Oh, that's harsh. You shouldn't have based your decision on how it was for your sisters." And it's true that when I was younger I felt shaky about my decision. However, as I've watched more of my friends become parents, and as I have become more entrenched in my profession, I'm now confident that my decision to remain childless is a sound one.

I think our society as a whole lacks mothering qualities. Nor is the role of motherhood given the respect it deserves. I believe that "mothering" should be performed by everyone.

I am childless, yet I ask myself, "Am I a mother?" Yes. I have been motherly with my nieces and nephews; in some ways, I get a chance to be motherly with my students. I probably have the best of both worlds.

Sadhna Datta has been teaching in British Columbia in the New Westminster School District since 1988. She graduated from Simon Fraser University in 1992 with a Bachelor's degree in education. Currently she teaches Grade 3. She and her twin brother were born in Nairobi, Kenya. She is one of six children and with her family lived in Delhi, India, and London, England, where she was schooled from ages 6 to 14. She and her mother moved to Vancouver in 1973.

who wants to be a mommy?

JENNIFER WISE

WITH THE POSSIBLE EXCEPTION OF THE DAY I TURNED 10, when my parents gave me the absolutely coolest red-and-white portable record player, my happiest birthday was my 40th. Symbolizing my exit from the child-bearing years, turning 40 would liberate me at last. I would finally be written off, I thought, as a dud breeder and left alone to live my life in peace, without apology, without ever again having to field that mildly shocked, subtly disapproving question, the one that always sounded so impudently irrelevant to me: "But—aren't you going to have any children?"

Well, I thought wrong. Advances in obstetrics, combined with my juvenile taste in clothes, have conspired to prolong such questions well into my 40s. So here it is, once and for all, for whoever wants to know— my answer, as true and honest as I could make it (and it wasn't easy). First, though, a few things about me, so that I'm not misunderstood: I revere my mother, adore my siblings and their kids, and have lots of friends. I also love my students, who (I see on ratemyprofessors.com) find me "cute, hilarious, and down-to-earth," as well as "awesome, passionate, and caring." In short, I ain't no heartless bitch. It's just that, given my experiences and my hyper-logical brain, certain conclusions were inescapable. One of them was that motherhood was not for me. And I reached it at age six.

ℒ Toronto, 1965. Two amusing, stylish parents, Danish Modern furniture, Topo Gigio, the little mouse on the *Ed Sullivan Show* — my sisters and I had it all. As three little bourgeoises-in-training, however, we lived a strangely divided life. On the clean (and miserable) side were all the tongue-moistened tissues and washcloths and nail-brushes, the endless dressing and fussing and fastening. And then there was everything else: frogs, ponds, fingerpaint and clay. All of them made life worth living, and all of them made you dirty.

Imagine our grubby faces, then, on the day we were presented with three shiny pink baby dolls in three white wicker cribs, fully accessorized with doll-sized versions of all the instruments of torture routinely applied to little girls like us: The Comb, The Frilly Dress, The Hair Barrette. Was this some kind of joke? Or maybe a test? Would you rather A) construct a secret tree house; B) perform all the songs from *Fiddler on the Roof* in head scarves; or C) spend the precious hours of your playtime wiping and burping a small plastic replica of yourself? I considered the options and concluded that only a dunce would choose to play mommy.

I kept such thoughts to myself for years. It did not escape my attention that many females did seem to want to play mommy, and that most became mothers when they grew up. Rather than being chided for their lack of imagination, they were praised, cooed over and in various ways rewarded for it. I suspected myself of weirdness or worse. Maybe I was defective? Maybe I wasn't a real girl? How could it be that the tedium which I considered beneath the notice of serious people was not only accepted as normal for women but glorified as supreme?

ℒ University of Toronto, 1984. I enrolled in a graduate course and discovered George Bernard Shaw. Hallelujah. Here at last was a thread of hope that I might not be a freak after all. Nearly a century before, Shaw, too, had asked who wants to be a mommy, and his answer, while more radical in its implications, was essentially the same as mine. I thought that people who wanted to be mommies were just retarded. Shaw thought that they were retarding the whole species.

Shaw argued that the job of mother, like the job of politician, is organized in such a way that the worst people, rather than the best, are almost guaranteed to apply. Electioneering, for example, is such an unscrupulous business that those with the fewest principles are most likely to succeed at it. And traditional motherhood constitutes such an abominable enslavement for women that only the most servile of females would ever consent to it. Shaw granted both institutions some merits, since there are many worse systems than electoral democracy and the bourgeois nuclear family. But he nevertheless noticed that both "put a premium on a want of self-respect in certain very important matters; and the consequence is that we are very badly governed and are, on the whole, an ugly, mean, ill-bred race."

Ouch. Shaw threw this left hook to motherhood in the preface to a play called *Getting Married*. Nobody today will be offended by his jab at politicians. The idea that a system that rewards personal ambition will tend to deliver corrupt leaders is as old as Plato, and the evidence for its basic truthfulness fills our newspapers daily. But Shaw's other idea—that motherhood is so debasing that only debased women would really take to it—is still pretty shocking. And what about the evolutionary part of his theory, that the general defectiveness of our breeders is hindering human progress? Well, there's no shortage of proof that *Homo sapiens* remains a very depraved species indeed (see, for example, the 20th century). But could a systemic preference within motherhood for second-rate persons really be to blame for this? Does child-bearing in fact repel the best and brightest females, keeping the gene pool free of their positive influence?

Shaw thought so, although not because he had anything against mothers or motherhood per se. Quite the reverse. As good a Victorian as the next guy, he viewed the production of children as, potentially, a woman's noblest contribution to society. But as one of the greatest feminists of all time, he also saw how badly organized the institution of motherhood was in his era. In 1907, when Shaw began *Getting Married*, women were sexually and economically dependent on, as well as legally subservient to, husbands. Having children in 1907 brought with it the absolute requirement for a woman to indenture herself to a man who, under law, was her lord and master, and from whom it was almost impossible to obtain a divorce. The price of motherhood was therefore simply too high for any self-respecting woman to pay.

Shaw noted that English society abounded with "women of admirable character, strong, capable, independent," who quite understandably found the conditions of Victorian marriage intolerable and chose to remain unwed and childless; but he also noted the irony that these were the very women entrusted by their communities with the nurturing, protecting and raising of young people, as teachers, headmistresses and nurses. In schools, hospitals and other public institutions, women with independent minds were valued, paid for their labour and treated as responsible adults. Let them only wish to bear children of their own, however, and they were suddenly expected to subject themselves to the whims of an overprivileged man, and work without wages as his personal slave for life. The inevitable result was the enforced barrenness of England's most superb women, women whose very fitness for child-rearing paradoxically guaranteed that they would refuse to give birth.

As reassured as I was to find my opinions confirmed by such a thoughtful, witty genius, there was one problem. Shaw was speaking about motherhood as it existed before the liberation of Western women had even begun. He was writing before women had the vote, equal access to education and to protection under the law—before the invention of the (birth-control) wheel! Shaw has the rare distinction among feminists, besides being male, of having lived to see nearly all his proposals for the betterment of women's lives fully implemented. His insistence, in *Getting Married* and elsewhere, on a woman's right to divorce, to sexual and economic independence, to an education, a job, time and money of her own and control over her body, are things that nobody (except religious nuts) begrudges women today. The reforms he called for are now constitutionally enshrined throughout the Western world. In view of all that had changed for women since his time, I realized that I might, in the end, have to deny myself the validation I'd found in Mr. Shaw. Maybe his salvo against motherhood was historically obsolete, as irrelevant to my generation as a diatribe against corsets.

But that's not how it looked to me. Coming of age in Toronto during the 1960s and '70s, I'd grown up cultural light years away from the Victorian London of Bernard Shaw. Women in my time enjoyed the rights of full citizenship and could even raise children on their own, free of the marital indignities that so offended Shaw. But eliminating the need for husbands had done little to change the nature of motherhood. In fact, where maternal fundamentals were concerned, it seemed that nothing had changed at all, and that motherhood, at least as practised in North America, was still constituted in such a way as to discourage women like myself from engaging in it. Albeit for slightly different reasons, Shaw's basic insight seemed as valid as ever.

In the first place, there was the sadism of the activity itself. By the time we reached the doll years, my sisters and I had had such a surfeit of strippings, wipings, powderings, pinnings, lacings, tyings and bracings that I was confident they'd join me in turning up their noses at toys that merely recapitulated the whole miserable business at one remove. To my stunned surprise, they liked 'em. To my mind, no self-respecting child would willingly participate in the suffocation, through fussing, of another child, even if that child was only a doll. My adult understanding of the psychology of role-playing says that such things are done in the name of mastery. But there are some activities so pointless and inhumane that they are not worth perpetuating in any form. Our fastidious management of babies, our "regular old hen" mothering, as Shaw puts it in *Getting Married*, is assumed to be "natural," but in fact it's intolerable to children. If they're strong, it sends them running for their lives from the nursery at the first opportunity; if they're weak, they internalize and then re-enact it on their own babies by cruelly overscrubbing them, too. And yet motherhood in North America apparently requires it. Just try taking your child out in public in a dirty condition. You'll be hissed out of the park by the other moms. They might even have you arrested. No, it was clear to me at age six that I'd sooner spend my adult days as a ditchdigger than go over to the enemy as a Mistress of Hygiene, wielder of the fearsome Q-Tip, the glinting Diaper Pin.

And then there was the appalling lack of variety, also more or less unchanged since Shaw's time. Having been fussed over as a baby, then fussing over baby dolls as a child, the "normal" woman in my world was expected to go on to devote the most productive years of her adult life to *more* babyish fussing. What kind of sentient creature could be content with such monotony? Given the freedom to do more various, more intellectually absorbing and more socially useful things, who would want to spend her whole life, essentially, in the nursery? At six I knew I'd rather be a hobo; at least there'd be a change of scenery from time to time. As it turned out, I became an artist, writer and professor of theatre history. My sisters had children.

𝒢 Toronto, London, Paris, Athens, La Pocatière, 1985–1989. Were our different destinies innate, or had we acquired them? Probably both. I know my impulse to cultivate my abilities felt as natural to me as my sisters' decision to cultivate their eggs did to them—more natural, in some ways, since both of them claimed that they'd never had an urge to breed until their husbands suggested it. But on the other hand, the children they produced, my nephews and nieces, were (and still are) miraculous, gorgeous, irresistible beings whom I loved instantly with a deep, primal protectiveness. When little David throws his rubbery arms around my leg the second I walk in the door, smiling up at me and saying my name, over and over; when Jack solemnly takes my hand and leads me to the desk where he has all his art supplies laid out, ready for us to pick up where we left off in our joint comic master-piece, *Attack of the Centipedes*—that is, whenever I visit with my sisters' children, I fall like Alice right down the rabbit-hole into the wonder-land of childhood and play, hilariously, for hours.

This kind of rapport with children turns out to be the prerogative of aunts, however. My older sister, the more driven of the two, once said of her mothering style, like a housekeeper ruling out windows, "I don't play." I soon found out why: the reality of child-rearing in our time and place makes playing with children virtually impossible for mothers. They're too exhausted. They're too busy feeding, clothing and organizing their children to ever have the chance, or the energy.

Had my sisters and I, like the characters we used to play in *Fiddler on the Roof*, still lived in the eastern European shtetl of our ancestors, in tiny villages where everything was within walking distance, where live-in extended families shared the duties of child-rearing and nobody had to be driven to hockey practice on eight-lane super-highways at 6:00 A.M., or be picked up from school every day in armoured SUVs, then maybe, *maybe*, motherhood wouldn't have looked so unappealing. Or if I'd grown up in France, where maternity benefits for mothers and fathers alike are idyllic, and reckoned in years. But on this con-tinent, as far as the eye could see, a mother was a lonely drudge and driver, condemned to a (minimum) 10-year sentence of near-solitary confinement in her house and car. Considering the added insult of isolation, this new purdah was worse than the old one.

And the experts agreed. From Betty Friedan in 1964 to Susan Douglas and Meredith Michaels in 2004, the motherhood mavens were unanimous: motherhood in North America is a "myth," a "chaos," a "contradiction" and a "shock." It's a thankless and impossible task likely to drive you stark raving mad—if, that is, you're lucky enough to escape being bedridden with post-partum depression. According to women who had been through it themselves, the gifts of motherhood included stupefying boredom, social isolation, stultifying menial chores, ignorance and disillusionment, not to mention a vastly increased risk of prescription-drug addiction. Such exposés, which had been flowing nearly all of my life, confirmed the worst fears of my childhood. As did the mothers I saw on the streetcar and in the stores. They looked like serfs of an invisible master, forced in public to perform simple, everyday tasks made virtually impossible by their burden of babies, bottles, blankets and bags. It was heartbreaking and horrifying at the same time, like something out of Beckett. Poor sweating wretches! Sure, I'd open a door or retrieve a fallen pacifier, but there was little I could do to improve their lives. I could, however, make better choices in mine. Motherhood was clearly no proper job for a woman who cherished her mental and physical well-being and valued her time.

Shaw had correctly diagnosed the need for women's liberation. But what he hadn't counted on was that women could be liberated for life without being liberated from motherhood. In the absence of free, universal daycare, the women of my generation were faced with the exact same choice as Shaw's corseted Victorians: will it be tedium and self-diminishment at home with children, or growth and self-fulfillment in the adult world? Only millionaires were exempt; the rest of us had to choose. For as the experiences of my sisters, friends and colleagues made clear, an ordinary person who tries to combine work and motherhood will soon be a gibbering wreck.

The sleep deprivation. The total lack of privacy, sex and quiet. The constant demands to do and say the same things, again and again and again. The relentless questions. The loss of control over one's routine, the inability to fulfill one's own needs. These are the tried-and-true techniques of human torture. What mothers suffer every day in the privacy of their own homes would be considered a violation of the Geneva Conventions were it inflicted on soldiers during a war. The working mothers I knew quickly succumbed. They were stressed to the limit of their humanity. Many were on antidepressants or tranquilizers; some were hearing voices. All were perpetually sick with child-borne colds and flu. My younger sister, once so musical and funny, was either rushing from one dull chore to another—pickups, drop-offs, shopping, errands, work, then another round of pickups and drop-offs—or she was sleeping, often right there in front of me, minutes after I'd come over to visit. She had no time to read, think, be alone. She felt guilty and inadequate as a mother when she left for work in the morning, and depressed and aggrieved when she came home at night. Like many women of her generation, she eventually tried to end the torment by giving up her job. (The experiment was not a success.)

Yes, civil rights for women had been long overdue, but it was equally obvious that caring for babies must necessarily prevent one from taking full advantage of them. How could a woman artist have any hope of fulfilling her potential if she spent her days barfing, nursing and monitoring the relative locations of scissors, hot stoves and tiny hands? How could she seriously expect to devote her life to exposing injustice as a journalist, or defending civil rights as a lawyer, or understanding the cosmos as an astronomer, without also working long hours, occasionally travelling far from home, often being absorbed or emotionally unavailable for days, months, maybe years at a time—in short, without being criminally negligent as a mother? Mother sea turtles may drag themselves ashore once a year, drop their eggs into a sandy hole and return to the sea without a backward glance, their maternal duties fulfilled. But human babies are not sea turtles. They require round-the-clock care, close supervision for years. Motherhood for humans is an intense and prolonged commitment. The idea that a person could be simultaneously devoted to two such full-time causes, to her children and her public work, say to original research or creation in the arts, sciences or professions, is just not realistic. (A producer of television news whom I've known most of my life confided to me recently, in tones of a startling revelation, that having children had definitely harmed her career in journalism. *Duh*.)

℘ Gabriola Island, Nanaimo, Victoria, Berlin, 1990-2000. Through my 30s, I struggled toward my dreams. I finished my dissertation, travelled, studied languages, exhibited and published my work. I gained professional competence, made a home for myself, earned money, tenure and promotion. I revelled in the joys of creation and discovery, and the rewards of teaching. But as my childlessness was starting to look irrevocable, those closest to me were panicking: this was all fine and good, but when was I going to have *children* already? The first time I ever saw my mother cry was when I told her I wasn't. After my father's death, I learned that yes, he'd been proud of my books and so on, but he'd died deeply disappointed that I hadn't had any kids.

Whence comes this idea that all women should reproduce themselves? Not from any biological necessity, that's for sure. On a global level, we produce millions more babies each year than we can possibly care for. According to UNESCO, we allow over 10 million children to die of poverty, war, malaria and other preventable diseases—every year. Ten million a year, 100 million a decade. That's a lot of surplus babies. Why was everyone pressuring me and other ambitious young women to drop everything we cared passionately about in order to churn out more, more, more little humans? There were several billion of us on the planet already. This senseless mania for baby-making always reminds me of that scene from the movie *Aliens*, in which the egg-laying mother alien just keeps relentlessly, rhythmically, brainlessly squeezing out her goopy killer-offspring, regardless of the fact that they're fatal to all other life forms. Yes, I heard the biological clock, all right, but it was ticking for Mother Earth. With every tick it said: "Stop breeding already! I'm full. If your need to feed, clean and swaddle is really that deep, adopt a child who needs the care. There are millions to choose from." No, the world didn't need my babies. What it needed, and urgently, was my restraint and my services—in education, research and advocacy, in helping to save and enrich the lives of the children we already had.

So if motherhood is good neither for individual women nor, at this moment, for the rest of the planet, who would still agree to sacrifice herself to it? Bernard Shaw might have nailed it: only those who lack the backbone to refuse. Conditions for mothers may yet improve. Universal daycare may one day be recognized, like universal health care, as essential for an equitable society. Or (God forbid) an epidemic may one day depopulate the Earth to the point at which we'll all have to roll up our rubbers and do our procreative duty. But until then, altruistic women with strong minds and free spirits might reasonably demur. After all, the raising of the next generation doesn't begin and end with the physical production of offspring.

Parents and children alike depend throughout their lives on the commitment and skill of all kinds of experts and professionals, people who have devoted their lives to the well-being of all the new members of society, to setting their bones and correcting their essays, to nurturing their talents and saving their lives. Motherhood continues to be sentimentalized as the ultimate social good a woman can do. But the fact is that catering to the needs of her own children generally prevents a woman from accomplishing the much greater good that she could be doing for society as a whole. Ten years of committed motherhood, and what has she achieved? Another houseful of battery-operated toys, another pair of pampered, overly clean children who will grow up viewing the central woman in their life as, to some degree, a domestic servant. Great. No wonder we don't evolve.

℘ Victoria, 2006. I'm proofreading this essay, working at the very table on which my mother served me all the beautiful breakfasts of my childhood, all those Bunnykin bowls of porridge with their rivers of milk and islands of brown sugar. I look around my study at the fruits of a life devoted to other kinds of service — evidence of the students I've inspired, my books and drawings, the contributions I've made to the university, the community, the world. I think about what all of these things cost me in terms of time and concentration, and I know that I couldn't have done any of them if I'd had kids to care for. Not having had to serve porridge, I've had the privilege of teaching history. I think about that maxim of Cicero's, that to be ignorant of what happened before you were born is to remain always a child. I agree. And because I've dedicated my life so far to lifting my students out of that ignorance by teaching them about the past, I feel that I've spent the last 10 years raising, not one or two children, but hundreds.

A while ago I saw a pair of nudibranchs in a nature show on television. They were locked in their famous mating battle, a violent encounter that would leave one of them defeated and impregnated. As hermaphroditic sea creatures, either one of them might have been made a mother. But, as the narrator explained, motherhood is a drain on one's time and energy, and neither one of them wanted to be stuck with it. Curling, rising and unfurling gorgeously in the blue-green water, they fought for the right to remain child-free.

From this genetic distance, the problem with motherhood is clear. (Even invertebrates know it's a drag.) In the human realm, however, algae blooms of piety still obscure the facts. No matter how bad the working conditions, no matter how overcrowded the planet, child-bearing continues to be romanticized as the duty and destiny of all normal women.

Taiga and Isabelle, my nieces, when you're old enough to read this: this essay is for you. You may not be as lucky as I was, to stumble on Bernard Shaw when you need him. What's "normal" depends on who you are. If you don't want to be a mommy, it won't be because you're selfish, freakish or unwomanly. It'll be because, like me, you considered your options and chose to do something else.

Jennifer Wise is an associate professor of theatre history at the University of Victoria. She is the author of *Dionysus Writes: The Invention of Theatre in Ancient Greece* and co-editor of *The Broadview Anthology of Drama.* Her students find her entertaining and stimulating; her friends find her a lively conversationalist who loves to debate. She also paints and sculpts.

performing motherhood

SMARO KAMBOURELI

For Maria Gilli

TAKE ONE

Thessaloniki, Greece, *circa* 1970.

"I would have killed myself, had you not been a girl," my mother said in a matter-of-fact tone.

She was arranging herself on a chair, winter coat draped over her back, one hand reaching out to catch a black glove falling to the floor, the other balancing her shopping bags against the table leg. It was an overcast and windy day—or perhaps the weather details are my invention, a reflection of the constricting tightness in my chest at hearing my mother's words. Perhaps it was the gloom or non-gloom of the sky, my mother's utterance and my shock at it—not nightfall—that have translated this incident into a twilight memory. "Twilight," Andreas Huyssen says, "is that moment of the day that foreshadows the night of forgetting, but that seems to slow time itself, an in-between state in which the last light of the day may still play out its ultimate marvels. It is memory's privileged time."

We were in a pastry shop, at the corner of Egnatia and Agia Sofia streets, right at the centre of Thessaloniki, a city famous for elegant patisseries. But this was not the kind of place one lingered at, like Tottis or Corfu, both on the promenade avenue, both with second storeys, wide balconies and expansive views of the bay and port, the cafés my friends and I, adolescents living downtown, frequented. This was a site for a brief respite between errands. I had never been there before, nor do I remember its name. It's long been replaced by the inescapable, it seems, golden arches.

We had finished getting me a pair of loafers and a V-neck Shetland wool sweater for the new school year. The next stop was the bookstore, kitty-corner to the pastry shop. We were only a block away from the apartment building where we lived; why did we need a break? Perhaps my mother had planned to unburden herself over dessert, to sweeten the anguish of what she wanted to share with me. Or perhaps her statement, coming out of the blue as it did, was an unpremeditated release of the strain she had been under. All I recall is the suddenness of her words and the contents of the shopping bags: a navy-blue sweater that was to last well into university and the black patent loafers, trimmed in red, certain to make an impression on my friends.

As for my response, there is nothing to remember about it, nothing to forget: where did my impetuousness, my penchant for swift replies, go? I did not give voice to my sudden surge of fear and anger. Instead, noting the paleness of her face that made the abundance of her freckles even more pronounced, I shrugged my shoulders, feigning nonchalance. And so that moment of pathos passed without comment.

I was 16 at the time; she was younger than I am now. It was a particularly difficult time in her marriage—her marriage, our family—a classic case of what has given mothers-in-law in some cultures a fairy-tale status, the kind of tale that is not fair at all, that can cause havoc until, through the intervention of a *deus ex machina*, things take an upswing.

But there was no divine, or other, intervention in our lives. We persevered, often going through lengthy periods during which we did not speak to my grandmother, distance a good antidote to her larger-than-life character. She was a voluptuous beauty, flamboyant, temperamental, irreverent, humorous. Predictable, yet volatile. A meddlesome woman. A woman whose presence alone demanded attention, the heart of any social gathering. A veritable femme fatale, she was already married to her third husband, a Clark Gable look-alike, when I was born. He was 15 years her junior, the only grandfather I was to know, a man I adored. Grandma Smaro's life had secrets that, 20 years after her death, we are still unravelling. She was the kind of woman to whom only a sprawling realistic novel can do justice. And she was, as far as I was concerned, a bad mother.

My mother was no match for Grandma Smaro: except for the lushness of her red hair, my mother was a self-effacing woman. Nor did my father know how to handle his own mother. Worse than that, despite his best intentions, he seemed to have no idea of how to negotiate his wife's and mother's roles in his life—the source of all the tension in our family. Trapped between these two female poles, and equally devoted to each of them, he was often at a loss. An earnest man with a deep sense of commitment to social issues, he began to keep his mother at bay only after she became a small *cause célèbre* in the local media. Then he began to try resisting her influence, on some public occasions even pretending that he didn't know her.

I remember when my father became the focus of media attention. As leader of the large union of railway employees in northern Greece, he was in the fifth day of a hunger strike, along with the rest of the executive members and a small group of other employees. The strikers' wives and children kept a vigil outside the union's building at all times, holding banners in support of their men's cause. My mother took me along with her a few times; I recall seeing my father and a few other men coming to the big windows to wave at their wives and children, to assure us that they were still on their feet, still determined to give the government a good fight—an image that never fails to flood my mind when I happen to walk past that building.

On the day my father experienced what he called his greatest mortification ever, my mother had dropped me off at Grandma Smaro's on her way to the union's building downtown. I was a little under the weather and was not in school. In a rare moment of solidarity, the two women commiserated over my father's well-being and political struggle. Subsisting only on water occasionally laced with lemon and honey, some of the older men had already reached a worrisome point, hence the media attention. I missed and worried about my father, but I recall feeling delight at the sight of my mother and grandmother kissing each other on both cheeks as they said their goodbyes. It was going to be a fun day, I thought.

Sure enough, my grandmother led me into her bedroom, a place stuffed with all kinds of little luxuries and beautiful things that my mother could never afford. Grandma Smaro began beautifying herself—applying makeup and lipstick, putting on her string of pearls and matching earrings, and donning one of her most sumptuous *robes de chambre* (an expression I've always associated with her), a black *crepe-de-Chine* affair, ankle-length, with gorgeous dragons embroidered in gold and red thread on the front and back, a robe I have inherited that has served me well as a last-minute costume for the occasional Halloween party. Made in Persia, it was a gift from her second husband, a wealthy man close to 30 years older than her, who had died during the Nazi occupation.

Now, she said, turning away from the mirror to look at me, off we go to the kitchen. You'll help me make a delicious and most nourishing soup.

In no time, the apartment was redolent with the aroma of chicken soup. Now, she said again, as the soup was still simmering, you've got to make a most important call.

She explained the details of the call clearly enough, but I stared at her, alarm bells already ringing. I was old enough to know that this was an important call, but a call that meant trouble.

You call, I told her.

How can I possibly call myself, sweetie? Remember? I've just had a heart attack, the doctor is still here and I may pass away at any moment. So, I'll dial the number for you, and you ask for your father. When he gets on the line, you tell him that he must come over right away if he wants to see his mother before she dies.

But I'll burst into tears when I hear his voice. I haven't spoken with him for days.

Even better, she said, and planted a kiss on my cheek.

I kept staring at her in disbelief, but I did as I was told.

She was right. Of course my father wanted to see his mother one last time, but he certainly was not going to jeopardize either the success of the strike or his reputation as union leader. So he arrived by taxi, accompanied by two other executive members, followed by a taxi containing three journalists. I don't know if my grandmother had counted on my father showing up with this entourage, hence her dressing up. My poor father almost fainted when he saw her. I can't recall what words were exchanged—with the journalists snapping photos and asking questions, my grandmother slicing bread and pleading with the men to have a bowl of soup, and me holding onto my father's pant leg, there was a lot of commotion. Neither my father nor his colleagues touched the food, but, under the circumstances, they agreed to have a sip of cognac, and so did the journalists.

The strike was resolved in favour of the strikers' cause a couple of days later. My grandmother filed away that embarrassing episode, along with her photograph in two newspapers, as evidence of her one and only political fight in the name of motherhood. She claimed it was her intervention that helped bring the strike to a positive end. I don't think my father ever forgave her; union leaders in Greece did not have mothers dressed in pearls and silk robes attracting media attention. It was over half a year before he saw or spoke to her again.

This was the kind of woman my mother had to contend with. Years later, after the day my mother announced to me her self-thwarted intentions, and after I had read enough Freud and Jung, I had the temerity to share with my father my now-informed view of my grandmother. Over the remains of Christmas dinner, the first Christmas I was spending with my parents after I had gone overseas for graduate studies, I announced that Grandma Smaro was a manifestation of the terrible-mother archetype, a woman who had translated her penis envy into power hunger, a castrating woman. Perhaps because this was an interpretation that seemed to my father as outlandish as the other feminist ideas I had been unleashing over that short holiday, or perhaps because he was still in denial about what his mother was capable of, we ended up having a row, my mother a silent witness. Grandma Smaro had been dead for four months, but she still held sway over us.

That day in the pastry shop, I was too self-absorbed, bewildered by what my mother had said, to give her the compassion she needed and deserved. Instead, I was overwhelmed with dismay at what it seemed to be a mother. My mother was, is, a paragon of altruism and sacrifice, while the other mother who was turning our lives upside-down was egotism incarnate. Soon afterwards, feeling trapped in the family turmoil, I started constructing my own family romance. Not in the classic Freudian interpretation, but in the sense that I rejected both models of motherhood that ran in my family. My future imaginings of myself did not include being a mother. As my mother often feared during my adolescent years, I was not just my grandmother's namesake; living in fear of what her mother-in-law's next round of antics would bring, she was easily alarmed by what she thought were signs of my proclivity to be different. "Different," in my mother's lexicon, was synonymous with "bad." And there were signs to suggest that I would carve the shape of my own life by being different, by steering clear of the pitfalls of motherhood.

I have come to think of that incident with my mother as the moment that gave birth to who I have become by not becoming a mother. Announcing in my last year at high school that I had no room in my life for marriage and motherhood—I did go for ritual and ceremony in those days—was no small feat. Greek culture was, and still remains in some respects, a culture in which marriage and motherhood were the twin concepts defining a woman's goal in life. My mother was apoplectic; my father said that I could always change my mind after I finished university. He was right, at least in some respects, for I did get married, but I have never become a mother. And it's a miracle— perhaps even proof that a *deus ex machina* might after all touch our lives now and then—that I never got pregnant.

TAKE TWO

Winnipeg, Canada, *circa* 1980s.

Married, and a stepmother. Closer in age to my two stepdaughters than I was to their father, I never presumed to become a second mother to them. Their father loved—loves—them to pieces, but, even in the early days of our relationship, I had a hard time imagining him as the father of the child I might have had. Motherhood was a possibility lurking in the background, rarely raised as a prospect.

As a graduate student, I was immersed in the theories, especially feminist theories, that were coming out right, left and centre. Phallogocentrism was a sweet word—the kind of candy you like chewing on until it's got no taste left and you spit it out. Chances were that when a young woman who studied feminist theory declared to her husband that she was about to stop ironing his shirts, she would do so by embarking on a passionate treatise about essentializing women and the construction of femininity. I wasn't as different as my mother had feared: this is precisely what I did.

Those were also the days when, despite or, more accurately, because of feminism, motherhood was enjoying a renaissance period. Demystified, it began to lose its sheen as cultural mythology. Now motherhood had a pressing materiality. It became a matter of labour—the hard, physical labour of mothering—that demanded recognition, restitution, sharing, both on the home front and in the public sphere.

I don't know what had been sprayed over Winnipeg that one summer in the early 1980s, but it seemed that overnight, all of my women friends, most of them fellow graduate students, got pregnant. And each pregnancy was a happenstance. From the recently divorced friend who had dined with her ex-husband to mark their divorce to another friend who was fleetingly smitten by a guest speaker at the university, they all got pregnant one after another, happily—albeit with some anxiety—anticipating motherhood. Flat-bellied, I stood out like a sore thumb. It must have been the only time in my life I wished I had more flesh on my bones.

I joined in with gusto. I organized baby showers, taught friends' classes when needed, stood by them during their pregnancies and after their babies arrived. I drank in the sweet-and-sour smell of babies' tiny bodies, got to learn how to balance them in the crook of my arm, listened for their burping after they were fed. But listening to some of these mothers was not an altogether cheerful experience. Of course they had changed; how couldn't they have? But there was a huge difference, I thought, between becoming a mother and coming to terms with the responsibilities motherhood entailed. I was troubled by the fact that some of them had started advocating motherhood as the only way for a woman to sublimate flesh—her womanly flesh, her female body.

I was a reluctant witness to this transformation, this total absorption of all the things these women were into one role, that of motherhood. I was prepared to accept that this was a temporary condition, that although their children would—should—always come first, my women friends would somehow gradually recover those parts of themselves they had put on hold. But some of them never did so. They were not interested in picking up their lives where they had left off. Instead, they were living the apotheosis of woman as mother.

It was an encore of my mother's practice of motherhood, albeit with some critical differences. Surely, my friends had more options and opportunities than my mother ever did. But, in my view, they had all given in to motherhood. What they desired as women was consumed by the demands placed upon them as mothers. And, strangely, they seemed to have little recourse to alternatives. Motherhood was a great seducer, inexorably demanding more and more, squandering these women's desires without recompense.

I was in my mid-20s then. And perhaps, deep down, it was more my fears about how I would have acted under the same circumstances than my friends' conversion to motherhood that made me decide not to have children. I never looked back, never regretted the decision.

ℒ TAKE THREE

In another place, another time.

I should have become a mother. Or I should have adopted a child. Unlike some of my women friends who, like me, defied motherhood, who don't want to be bothered with children, I love children. I seek them out. And there is no end to my delight at being an aunt. Claudia, my brother's first child, changed my life. Hyperbole? I don't think so, though I'd be hard-pressed to explain how and why without resorting to clichés. I didn't think I could love another child as much, so I was nervous when my brother and his wife announced they were expecting a second baby. I confessed my fears to my mother, and she had a good laugh. When Christina—and later Iason—was born, I was head-over-heels in love all over again. My anxiety these days is that, as they're maturing fast, I may end up becoming peripheral in their lives. But

Iason, who has just turned 10 (the only one of the three interested in my life, who tells me I should work less and still likes having sleepovers at my place), assures me I worry needlessly.

TAKE FOUR

A large classroom at the University of Victoria, *circa* December 1987.

She hasn't washed her beautiful long hair for days. She's got dark rings under her eyes. As she looks down at her exam booklet, her hair cascades over her face. She hasn't written a word for 10 minutes now. She's chewing on her pen, her foot tapping the floor. As she goes over the examination sheet once again, her lower lip quivers.

I want to go over to her, pat her back, squeeze her hand, tell her that it's okay, that, even though she may fail the exam, she can still pass the course, that even failing a course is not the end of the world. But I can't. I am her teacher.

Pedagogy has always been affiliated with nurturing—and with a certain kind of erotics. But body contact is a no-no, at least in most cases. Yes, you can hug a student to congratulate him or her on successfully defending a thesis, but pedagogy has its own rules of intimacy. We must strive to understand what goes on inside our students' minds, but their bodies must remain beyond our reach. Intimacy as a pedagogical strategy is a dangerous one, understandably so. It's difficult to practise closeness in the professional space; the terms of engagement are constantly under negotiation. But I cannot help but feel maternal toward my students. And this is more than a maudlin feeling; it goes beyond a mere pedagogical stance—rehearsing devotion to the profession of teaching, seeing teaching as a vocation.

Perhaps it is because I don't have children that I don't resist the energy and effort this takes: being there for them when they're about to break down, when they want someone to believe in them if everything else about the system fails them, when they need to be pushed to give all they've got. The irony is that I don't think my students perceive me as maternal; if anything, the adjective that recurs most often in my teaching evaluations is "intimidating"—a definition of my pedagogy that clashes with my self-image as teacher, that never fails to shock me. So, I take performing motherhood in my pedagogical life to be my secret, a secret role that sustains me professionally, that gives some shape and meaning to the frenzy and pressures of being a university teacher today.

ℒ TAKE FIVE

Geniki Cliniki, Thessaloniki, *circa* October 2001.

The snow keeps coming down, quietly yet relentlessly. It is so thick that all I can see through the window of my father's room at the clinic is a shimmering whiteness—only the gold light of the neon sign on the building across the street flickers through. Despite my exhaustion, I feel stirred by excitement. My body remembers the thrill of missing a day's school on the rare occasion of heavy snow while I was growing up in this city; the snowstorm that turned a first date in upstate New York into a 22-year marriage; the blizzards in Winnipeg that I revelled in; the whiteouts on the prairie highways.

I want to tell my father, remind him that he offered to send me a return ticket to Greece the first time I told him that it was -35° in Winnipeg. But when I turn to face him, his eyes are closed, and I decide not to disturb him. I listen to his heavy, irregular breathing, look at his sunken cheeks, his crooked moustache—the result of my feeble attempts at playing barber—under the oxygen mask, the IV tubes, the half-full urine bag. His body, emaciated, eaten up by cancer, has turned into a cyborg, a hybrid of machines and brittle bones, the only way of staying as comfortable as possible under the circumstances.

The suction machine used earlier today is still in the room, evidence of the third close call in two weeks. The doctors have already warned me that we may lose him any time now. Lose him? I objected to their use of the word. They were patient with me; they've come to indulge my demands for a more exact language, for more details about their predictions, more informed explanations of the cancer-treatment options I have to consider. I am, one of them declared one day, the most informed caregiver they have encountered aside from those who are related to the medical profession. I owe this to my (ex) stepdaughter in the States who regularly emails me recent updates on prostate and bone cancer treatments and painkillers. Being informed is one way of staying sane, of remaining in control, of knowing that all that can be done for him is being done.

Recently, I've started to detect in my behaviour what, I'm certain, has already been apparent to others around me, the desperation that keeps me on my literally on my toes. I'm jumpy, constantly on alert. Even when I'm catching some sleep on the other bed in his room, or sleeping stretched over adjoining chairs, I'm always ready to leap up at the slightest stir or moan. Even with the arrival of the private nurse we hired to give my mother and me a break, I still linger. The time he has left is so little, so precious, I leave the clinic only when it is absolutely necessary. Sometimes, late at night, when he is asleep or heavily drugged, I walk to one of the cafes or bars along the avenue to get a takeout Scotch or cross the street to stride briskly along the promenade. The sea is usually calm. The cargo ships anchored in the middle of the bay and the couples necking in the dark of the night often take me by surprise: there is life outside the ward of acute cases. Looking at the lights of the city on the other side of the bay, I realize that Geniki Cliniki has become my polis within a polis. For seven months now, I've had no life beyond that of taking care of my father.

Taking care of him has long gone past helping him walk to the bathroom or giving him his medication. In the last four months, I've turned into the main custodian of his body. The more it wanes, the more involved I become with its painful lived experiences, its various secretions. From holding the bedpan for him to putting him in diapers, from entertaining him with stories while coaxing him to eat to feeding him, from helping him get into clean pajamas to giving him a sponge bath, my father's body has become more familiar to me than the body of a lover. Its nakedness is no longer taboo to his daughter's gaze, to the touch of her fingers. My father has become all body, an abjected body, a body inscribed by his history, remembering his life story in fits and starts.

When I arrived at the clinic at 6:30 A.M. two days ago, Noonoo, the private night nurse we hired a week ago, an Armenian immigrant from Georgia, told me that he had been very agitated all night and had to be restrained. That did not surprise me. The cocktail of drugs he has been on has caused some disturbing episodes of paranoia. We had him strapped to the bed once before—partly because he attempted to attack a nurse he thought was about to kill him, partly because he removed his oxygen mask and pulled away one of his IV drip tubes. His doctors and I were scheduled to meet later that day to discuss other treatment options.

He was moaning again when Noonoo left. When I bent over to kiss him on the forehead, he pushed me away with as much force as he could muster and started sobbing. It was not his sobbing that caught me unawares; I had seen him cry before, begging us to take him back home. What took my breath away was the word he cried out again and again in his feeble voice: "Mama, Mama, Mama."

I climbed into the bed and took him in my arms. I held him as tightly as I dared—his bones could collapse at the slightest abrupt movement or firm touch. "There, there," I kept whispering, while rocking him softly. After a while, he fell asleep in my arms. A daughter become mother, performing motherhood: an ambivalent performance for many reasons, not least of all for my impersonation of Grandma Smaro.

ℒ CODA

Guelph, *circa* November 2005.

Why is it that we tend to associate caregiving and devotion with motherhood? Why do we so often resort to maternal metaphors to talk about doling out unqualified love? There is no easy, let alone quick, answer to these questions. But one thing is certain in my mind: in the public imagination, motherhood embodies an incarnation of origins and therefore remains caught between nature and culture. Despite all the changes we've witnessed in society in the past century, motherhood is a sign whose meanings we're still trying to fathom.

When I perform motherhood, I do not seek compensation for not being a mother. I do not rehearse something I lack. Motherhood, in this case, is a trope, an analogy that shows how heavily inscribed maternity is in the course of our lives, in the cultural paradigms that shape us.

Smaro Kamboureli is Canada Research Chair in Critical Studies in Canadian Literature at the University of Guelph. Her publications include *Scandalous Bodies: Diasporic Literature in English Canada*. She has just completed *Making a Difference: Multicultural Literatures in English Canada,* a new edition of her anthology *Making a Difference: Canadian Multicultural Literature.*

sweet nothings

SARAH LEAVITT

WHEN I WAS IN HIGH SCHOOL, I used to have nightmares that I was pregnant. My belly would start bulging with an alien mass; when I tried to go get an abortion, it would turn out to be too late. While other girls were fantasizing about having babies, I was waking up screaming.

I stopped having pregnancy nightmares after a few years, but I never made it onto the baby bandwagon, aside from a few brief moments that my one and only boyfriend and I spent fantasizing about round, perfectly formed, happy babies that would someday join us to make a family. After he and I broke up, I came out as a lesbian. The girls back home in Fredericton, New Brunswick, were having babies. But I had daringly moved to Vancouver and was busy going out to dyke bars all night, marching in political demonstrations and, as often as possible, having brief, tormented trysts with inappropriate women. Babies were the last thing on my mind. How could I have known that my queer refuge was about to be infiltrated?

The invasion started out small. In 1993, a lesbian friend began trying to get pregnant. She did it the old-fashioned way: the donor was a gay guy she knew and whenever she was ovulating, he would jerk off in a baby-food jar. Then my friend's girlfriend would race to his apartment in the West End, pick up the warm jar and rush it home to Commercial Drive. My friend inserted the semen with a syringe and propped her feet up on the wall to help things along. She got pregnant after a couple of months. I was invited to the birth, along with the two midwives, the girlfriend and assorted other friends.

The birth was thrilling; right afterwards, I phoned the dyke bar and told the bartender, who passed on the news to everyone there. I developed an abiding love for my friend's baby, a doted-on anomaly in our crowd of 20-something lesbians. There weren't any negative consequences from the birth that I could see, aside from times when I wished my friend still went to bars or when I agreed to babysit and ended up missing out on parties where there might be cute girls. Small nuisances.

Only years later did I begin to get scared of babies again. This was around the time of Y2K and 9/11, when my friends and I reached our mid-30s and all of a sudden everyone seemed to start losing their minds. All of them, even the most rebellious, environmentally conscious, queerest dykes, began declaring their intention to have babies. Should I have been alerted by the stock-market investing and house purchasing, the master's degrees and the shaved legs? In any case, I was caught off guard when the procreation race began. The sheer numbers of women rushing to reproduce started me thinking about the scary, even nightmarish, consequences of making babies.

The first step for lesbians has to be the search for a donor. Who is the ideal donor? Well, for my white, middle-class friends, he is white, middle-class, able-bodied, smart, successful, fit and healthy. Musical, artistic, yet with a sensible job. Why is this scary? Right. Nothing scary about genetic engineering, no undertones of classism or racism, creation of a perfect Aryan master race, or playing God? Many of my friends, because they were older, needed costly interventions such as fertility drugs or in vitro procedures. They ended up spending thousands of dollars in addition to what they'd already laid out for frozen sperm. What about adoption, I wondered. Oh no, they said. It's just as expensive. And the available babies are so fucked up. And you know, I just really want one of my own.

I can't help thinking that there's a creepy sort of arrogance in the need to create more of your own flesh and blood, and in the assumption that this is a good thing. Some expectant couples attempt to portray their actions as altruism. Their baby will make the world a better place. People "like us"—left wing, well educated—are the people who should be having babies. Our babies will grow up to be tolerant and smart, and they will recycle. Right. Of course, there is no chance that a baby raised by nice lefty parents will turn out to be conservative or an asshole or abusive or murderous. No chance that she will be poor or sick or depressed. Or that she will live into a future of war and disease and unrestrained capitalist mayhem that she can do little about. Do my lesbian friends, not to mention the millions of hetero-sexuals determined to reproduce at any cost, know that a Canadian baby will grow up to pollute the world and produce garbage at a rate hundreds of times greater than a baby in the developing world?

And to be frank, aside from the environmental damage, one can-not ignore the damage to otherwise interesting women. When my friends decide to get pregnant, we begin the constant discussion of donors and fertility problems, then morning sickness and pregnancy diets, then diapers and schools and sleeping schedules. Discussions of baby-related topics can consume a room of women in seconds. If only paintings or manuscripts or other acts of creation were given equally intense attention.

Announcements of conception, pregnancy or birth invariably cause a frenzy of celebration. A negative or even neutral response is unthinkable. Wonderful, we dutifully exclaim when a friend conceives or even when someone we don't know conceives—say, a friend of a friend, or a daughter of a friend. When someone has a baby, we are expected to be overcome with a frantic desire to see it, to buy it things, to go into convulsions over its cuteness. Unimaginable (inconceivable!) that we would say, "Why on earth would you have a child when there are already so many living who need parents and homes?" Or, "I wish you wouldn't add to the population that is decimating our planet." Or perhaps, "It's not fair to bring a child into a world led by madmen where any social safety net will most likely be gone by the time they need it." What if we said, "I'm not interested in babies." Or, "I don't think your baby is smart or cute"? What if we suggested our friends get a pet or find a hobby instead of trying to conceive? But no. Any of these responses would expose us as hard-hearted, bitter and, worst of all, selfish. I have never understood how it is selfish not to have a baby.

One of the strongest forces that push women to have children must be the desire to exercise our magical ability to create something where there was nothing. To create a human, for God's sake, this complex, miraculous creature. Sure. I get it. It's not like I've never felt this urge myself. In 1998 my mother was diagnosed with a terminal illness. For the next six years, until she died, I started returning to Fredericton several times a year to visit her and my father. During my visits, I would find myself surrounded by my high school friends who were married and contented, amply supplied with chubby blond children. They went to the farmers' market on weekends and breathed clean country air. I started to think that maybe I could be straight and get married to one of the polite, athletic boys I'd known in high school. I would buy a heritage house and have a herd of kids. And my mother was dying. She loved children, and I could have one that looked like her, that was my and her flesh and blood. As she had done, I could read them books, feed them healthy food, sew them clothes. I grew restless with my writer/student/activist life in Vancouver; it seemed immature. After these visits, I would come back to the city and fight with my tattooed, pierced artist-girlfriend.

I dreamed of a safe, warm life far from the margins. I imagined my later life as a lonely and bitter place if I did not reproduce. When my mother was ill, her children helped care for her. We had moments of indescribably intense love and connection with her, of beautiful nurturing and sacrifice. When my grandfather died, he was surrounded by his children and grandchildren, all adoring and proud of being related to him. I should have babies, I thought, bring sparkle and joy into my life, fend off a future alone in a tiny cold apartment. I imagined myself in my 50s and beyond, when my friends would bring me photos of their children and grandchildren, enumerating their successes, pitying my solitude.

Luckily I came to my senses and remembered that I really *really* do not believe that creating more humans is an ethical choice at this point in our history. And I thought about who I really was. I remembered my friends, who have always been the most valuable thing in my life, my partner (who might not die tragically before I do) and my students and other children whom I care for and who may be there for me when I am old. I remembered—insane that I could ever forget—that I am certainly not straight, and that I am most at ease living in a big dirty city, writing and making art.

Lately I keep thinking about the term "sweet nothings." That seems to be the only thing that anyone wants to hear when they're talking about making babies: congratulations, I'm so happy for you, that's wonderful. But there's another reason why these two words keep spinning around my mind. Before a baby is conceived, there is nothing. And that nothing is sweet. It is a perfect imaginary baby, made in the likeness of its parents, happy, healthy and good. It is not a child who is different from them or whom they don't like. Not a disabled child or a depressed child or a child who wishes all the time that she had never been born at all. Those who want to have babies are longing for sweet nothings, imaginary people who do not yet exist. Although determined procreators (and various religions) speak of souls just waiting for the right parents to give them concrete form, I can't buy this idea. Parents dream of sweet nothings, and then they make the nothings into something.

When people reproduce, they are creating new human beings to fulfill their own hopes and dreams and needs. I wish that they would stop and think about their potential babies and what it means to make them real. I dream of potential parents turning away from these sweet nothings and giving their love and energy to bittersweet somethings: to the children who already exist on this planet, to their own needy or neglected selves, to the forests and oceans and rivers that have been damaged by generations of humans. Then perhaps the mad rush of reproduction would end. The baby nightmares would be over.

Sarah Leavitt regularly contributes writing and comics to *Geist* magazine and writes a monthly column for *Xtra West*, Vancouver's lesbian and gay newspaper. She has created short documentaries for CBC Radio and her articles have also appeared in *The Globe and Mail* and *Vancouver Review*, as well as a number of anthologies. She is working on a graphic novel.

how weird is that?

HANNAH MAIN-VAN DER KAMP

THERE'S JUST A CRACK OF LIGHT between the curtains, and I'm drowsily stirring when she flings the door open and lands beside me on the bed.

"So," she says, "say some more about the God thing."

A visiting niece, early 20s, glowing with the sweat of a morning run. Propping herself on an elbow, she pokes me in the ribs, "Hey, Antenna, my friends think I'm loonie because I give toonies to homeless people, like you do. I say to my friends, you think that's weird? My aunt makes her dogs sit for prayers before they eat! Wake up, Antenna, time for some more weirdness coaching."

"Antenna," short for Aunt Hannah, wonders for a moment if "weird" could be some kind of compliment.

It never occurred to me that I would not have kids. The possibility did not come up in my conversations with my husband-to-be or with friends and sisters. That I would conceive and give birth was assumed. Married at 25, I was in my early 30s when I began to realize I was never going to have children. Why? It's a long story and not my focus here but to say it involved tears, anger, prayers, threats, hopelessness and helplessness would be an understatement. There are many explanations but no good ones. When I've had a little too much to drink and am holding my sisters' grandchildren, I still have to swallow. But my life has, nevertheless, been child-filled. I've lost track of the number of great-nieces and -nephews whose photos I keep on fridge and desk. My husband and I were group home parents in the 1970s. For years, I experienced professional fulfillment as an elementary school teacher. My husband and I are legal guardians and godparents. As I age, another role begins to shape me. Being a childless aunt places me in a unique and privileged position.

I'm not a B&B hostess, not a fairy godmother, not just a source of cash and gifts, neither a therapist nor a teacher, not a spiritual guide, not a guru, not a shaman. Some of those aspects are present at times, but the role has another name on which I cannot quite put my finger: "oddness coach" or "eccentricity mentor" will have to do. It's not incidental that I am childless; not being a mother has given me the time, resources and courage to let my life and work unfold along unpredictable paths, to include eclectic passions. I had no young of my own to protect, no camouflaged nest to secure.

It's not my intention to prove that "life-of-a-childless-woman-can-be-good." There are plenty of examples of that, although the prevalence of young, infertile women desperate to conceive seems to be on the increase. Our culture is so conflicted! Abortion on demand lives next door to demand for publicly funded fertility clinics. Somebody should have told us decades ago that splitting fertility off from sexuality brought women reproductive freedom with a price tag.

My role has to do with oddness. Though I am able to appear relatively normal, and I know how to socialize in consensus reality mode, the truth is, *I am a little strange.* I don't carry all my belongings around in bags and I do not keep a dozen cats, but my compost boxes have a higher value for me than an ancient laptop. A few weeks ago, reluctantly, I had to retire my much-ridiculed, 30-year-old, clunky television set. Except to use their washrooms, I haven't been in department stores for a decade or two. In a box store once, and that under duress, I experienced vertigo. My clothes (previously owned, of course) are purchased for the quality of the textiles, not the fashion. Yes, I "say grace" with my dogs before I feed them their raw beef and turkey necks; why not? Worse, I write poetry and read it aloud to captive audiences. And I'm religious; a candlelit church filled with Gregorian chant is more pleasing to me than a social event graced by sequins and champagne. The principles of homeopathy thrill me. Our dinner guests are enjoined to drink a concoction of apple-cider vinegar and honey before they eat. Four months of the year, I swim in the ocean every day. Bed and shower are the only places where I do not wear binoculars around my neck.

Did I mention the daily consumption of fresh organic garlic? The dream journal? A tendency to light incense and paint mandalas in the small hours may seem only a little peculiar, but not believing in the germ theory of disease—how weird is that?

Not quite weird enough, it seems, for my nieces, nieces-in-law, goddaughters, daughters of friends and great-nieces—because they're asking for more. While their visits, emails and phone calls interfere with my reclusivity (probably a healthy interference), our bonding and enjoyment of each other grows steadily. I need them to balance my life; their affection and generosity I know will be there for me even if I do become a bag lady. They seem to need me because there isn't enough weirdness around in urban, middle-class culture.

Who doesn't have peculiarities? What we lack is enough safe places in which to reveal and revel in them. Childlessness has historically been associated with strangeness, sometimes as an idealized spiritual model but more often viewed negatively. Patriarchal attitudes cling; women who do not reproduce may easily become objects of scorn and mistrust. Infertile women often suffer a sense of being incomplete.

They are expected to behave hysterically. They also have a long tradition of defying authority; for example, 17th-century "witches." Had I been born in that century, most likely I would have been assigned the role of "hag," living on the outskirts of a settlement, stirring my pease porridge over a smoky fire. Knowledgeable about the reproductive process and its prevention, skilled in midwifery, I'd be sought out for cures and oracular utterances. Though my present role as an older-generation guide and companion is rich, I realize others still consider it to be second-best.

Four aspects of my role warrant exploration. The first is as a buffer between parents and their children. Every parent-child relationship needs rough spots. Individuation and the development of personal resilience requires disengagement from the parent. For teenagers, that usually includes open conflict. Good. But only if there are places where the teen can go and be accepted unconditionally. I've had to struggle with this because I'm prone to take sides and conflicted by loyalty to my siblings. Over the years, our guest room has been taken over by kids who, for one reason or another, temporarily could not live with their parents. I hope that my husband and I would be just as hospitable if we had kids of our own; many parents of teens are. However, the fact that there are no other children in our home ensures that the visiting youngster has no competition for our attention—and don't we all need to be an only child once in a while?

The second aspect is "dreaming together." I'm not referring to fantasy or daydreaming or to nighttime dreams, but to the capacity for being alert in the moment to inexplicable occurrences, synchronicities, stubborn symptoms, fleeting body sensations and deep yearnings which we have been trained to disavow. Our culture places a high value on productivity, technological aptness and financial acumen. I offer a counterpoise: dreamy states, voluntary moderation and slowness. There is nothing inherently wrong in being a financially secure, organized and focused person except when that is all there is, consuming all the psychic energies.

Most young people who relate to me have abandoned traditional religious practice. They certainly experience the Divine, the eternal Energy, the great Mystery but may not use the noun "God" to describe those experiences. Why they consider that word inadequate and how secularism has replaced historical religion is fascinating but beyond the scope of this discussion. Secular or religious, we all need those altered states to impart balance to sequential, verbal and goal-oriented lives. Dreaming, the domain of young children, artists and many of those who have "mental health issues," is necessary for personal and communal health. As I get older, more of my daytime hours are spent in slight trances. I make no apologies for that.

When I have guests, I excuse myself to practise meditation or contemplative prayer. My cold-water-loving Labs keep me walking entranced beside the sea most days. Recording dreams upon awaking prolongs hypnogogia. I try to write a poem daily (mostly a line or two), and may need to miss meals, phone calls and drop-ins if I have not spent the time required for gazing at clouds or chickadees while waiting for the poem event. The young men and women who call or stay know and respect this. I hope they value it in their own too-busy social and vocational lives.

I am not hoping for emulation; that's vain. What I hope to be, flawed as I am, is an indicator that another way of living is possible. Does one have to be childless in order to be a model of slowness? No, there are mothers who do this very well; my own mother did while she raised nine children in relative poverty. She had her daily gazing times, would go to a favourite upstairs window with a cup of tea and close the door. Could I have escaped the frantic busyness of an urban middle-class lifestyle if I had become a mother? There's the rub; I think not. I know my own weakness: quick to give in to pressure and expectations. Though some mothers can do it, I doubt I could have. So there, in a roundabout way, is a partial answer to the question of what God had in Her mind when She gave me my conception-less life.

The third aspect is the challenge of "doing my own work in public." Most of the young people who are related to me have known me since their early childhood. Believe me, they know my faults. A nephew recently told me that one of the biggest shocks in his early years was accidentally overhearing Antenna saying "swear words" to her husband. Being intimate requires admission of faults and fears, dreams and hopes. I speak openly about my unattractive obsession with trivial possessions, my insecurities, my religious doubts and the difficulties in my marriage. There is a place for discretion, and I hope I am being appropriate, but secretiveness I try to detect and avoid. Without degenerating into prurience, mutual trusting openness leads to the most intimate conversations about sexuality, spirituality, addictions, abuse, death and love. If I can do my self-talk out loud in the presence of young people I love, then perhaps it gives them permission and courage to do the same, for their well-being and the well-being of the world.

Lastly, my role as a quirky aunt encourages me to dwell on and heighten "peak" experiences, both my own and others'. There is a communal amnesia in families, religious congregations, schools and workplaces. When something Really Big happens, it registers as a thrill; but there is a simultaneous converse pressure to erase the big experience quickly, disavow, ignore and bury it. Get on with the sameness routines. Uniformity does not make allowances for shattering events; it distrusts ecstasy and terror. Have your big feelings and strong opinions if you must, but keep them to yourself. You've had a "cancer experience"? Fine, tell us about it, once, but keep your recurring anxieties private. Are you grieving a death? In public, please do it minimally.

As my hard-earned reputation for nuttiness allows me, and as I have the courage to do it, I try to amplify the powerful occurrences by bringing them to awareness again and again: car accidents, house fires, serious illness, deep love, enmities and inexplicable aversions. Noticing new bits of information, I ask to hear the story one more time. Should a childless woman be more able to elicit crucial experiences than a mother? Again, not necessarily, but I have the time, am relatively unbiased and can take bigger risks. Some things one does not recount to one's mother; then it is good to have another accessible ear.

It's a role that I suspect most mothers cannot and should not take on. Mothers have other tasks. Although unconventional mothers certainly exist, I suspect most children want a "normal" mother so they can bring their friends home without embarrassment. Somebody has to teach the skills required for living contentedly within the culture of convention without rocking the boat; at the same time, someone else needs to be questioning those conventions. The whole human family suffers when diversity is repressed. Risking contempt and scorn, I am compelled to take some small steps to transform the epidemic of blandness. Together, we can challenge and change the culture. It's a kind of social activism. The pressure on young women to conform to artifice, consumption and promiscuity is subtle but overwhelming. Let every church have a Hildegaard of Bingen! May every political body include several Nellie McClungs! Put an Eleanor Roosevelt behind every beauty counter! Barring that, may every girl have a peculiar aunt.

Peculiar does not mean misanthropic. Neither am I lauding the anguish of schizophrenia or the roller coaster of bipolar disorder. Eccentricity is not an excuse for obstinacy or self-indulgence. I need frequent reminders of that; fortunately, my husband obliges. A well-balanced eccentric inhabits the role totally and authentically. I've lived in England for periods and noticed that, although the English have a low tolerance for diversity ("not the done thing"), they cherish their eccentrics, those individuals for whom oddness is not an aberration but their true nature. There is an unstated agreement in rigid societies that uncanny and unpredictable persons are a corrective in the way that nighttime dreams are compensatory, providing access to what is overlooked in daytime reality. When I reluctantly first noticed that my own extended family had attached the epithet "crazy" to my name, I was hurt. Slowly I came to the realization that it is an assigned role and that the role suits me. If I hadn't been able to pick it up, the family would have had to assign it to someone else, perhaps someone less able than myself to be "crazy." Being the only childless adult, I was the preferred candidate.

Recently I had the honour to do The Reading from Christian scriptures at a family wedding. I took a few liberties with the text and, at my age, I probably should not have worn a fringed and beaded shawl: risky behaviours at a happy but solemn event. Afterward, one of the young women (not a church attender) exclaimed, "Antenna, if you ever start up your own church, I'm joinin' it!" That's enough affirmation to keep me unconventional for the rest of my life, although I have zero call to start a church.

A different niece in a city far away phones. "Help!" she says. "How do I keep white fluff from adhering to my black parka?"

"Anti-static spray," I reply.

"I'll do it," she says, "and by the way, do you believe in life after death?"

My answer is affirmative. I ask her what she's thinking. We talk about resurrection, reincarnation, near-death, the white fluff, God, funerals, static. Before she hangs up, she says, "Thanks, Antenna, I can ask you anything."

How sweet is that?

Hannah Main-van der Kamp is a poet, reviewer and columnist with four published books to her credit. *According to Loon Bay*, her most recent book, was published by St. Thomas Press, Toronto. She lives in Victoria, B.C., but with her husband and dogs spends part of the year on the mainland, several deep fjords north of Vancouver, blissfully free of modern communications/interruptions.

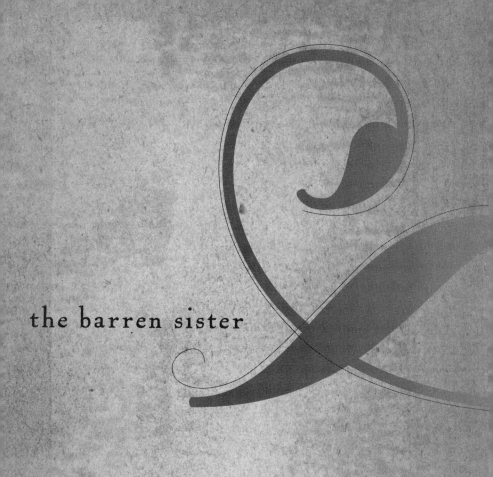

the barren sister

ADRIENNE MUNRO

"Instances of barrenness are noticed." —*Easton's 1897 Bible Dictionary*

AS A CHILDLESS WOMAN, I often come face-to-face with questions of identity. I am one of 10 cousins; collectively, we have produced 22 offspring—a healthy average of 2.2 children each (a 23rd is on the way). I am one of three sisters; between us, we have produced three offspring—a slightly more modest accomplishment. In either case, I lower the average. Of the 10 cousins, of the 3 sisters, I am the only one without children, the only one who has not borne fruit. I am the end of the line. A dead-end street. The lone withered branch on the family tree. I am the Barren Sister.

At least, that's how I have referred to myself over the years. The Barren Sister. In jest, of course. I didn't mean anything by it. In this very writing I had intended to discuss this state of barrenness, this void, this something I lacked. But the act of sitting down to write about it has instead compelled me to examine my "barren" status more closely.

A quick review of online dictionary definitions for the term "barren" reveals its implications for the childless woman—"providing no shelter or sustenance"; "incapable of sustaining life"; "an uninhabited wilderness that is worthless for cultivation"; "the trackless wastes of the desert." Synonyms range from "bleak, desolate and stark" to "unproductive, fruitless, unprofitable and empty." Shakespeare was kind enough to furnish us with the additional interpretations of "mentally dull" and "stupid." And from *Easton's 1897 Bible Dictionary,* "For a woman to be barren was accounted a severe punishment among the Jews," and "Instances of barrenness are noticed."

By self-identifying as barren, I have unwittingly been subjecting myself to the baggage of the ages, the nastiness accorded generations of childless women around the globe—and proliferating the concept of woman as vessel, useful for nothing but procreation. An update to my outlook seems in order.

Perhaps I should state for the record that I am not unable to have children, but have chosen not to. This is in no way an anti-child stance; on the contrary, I adore children. Nothing in my background easily explains my decision to remain childless, if indeed explanation is required. I come from a close-knit, loving and stable family. When I grew up in Kamloops, a medium-sized town in the interior of British Columbia, I enjoyed an idyllic childhood—hot, dry summers, cold, snowy winters and lots of friends and family around. I developed a strong sense of community—we moved only once, when I was four, to a home no more than two kilometres from our previous residence. We knew our neighbourhood, and we knew our neighbours. My parents live there still.

Despite this sense of community, I developed itchy feet. When I turned 18, I moved to Toronto. The following year I packed off to attend university in Charlottetown, Prince Edward Island. In subsequent years I moved and travelled frequently, working in museums, on archaeological projects and sometimes at uninteresting jobs in interesting locales, always endeavouring to own no more than I could fit into my van. But something changed when my first niece was born: I realized that I was too far away from her.

I returned to complete my studies in British Columbia and made frequent trips to Kamloops to see my family and spend time with my niece. I continued my forays into the wider world, but never for long. Soon my second niece was born, and a few years later I was present for the birth of my third. My connection with these children has completely changed my life, my priorities, my way of seeing the world. I love them beyond words. I see them and take part in their lives as much as I can. As I watch them grow and change, I am overwhelmed by the kinds of joy and wonder and heartache that only children can inspire.

Why on earth, you may ask, would I not want children of my own?

Making the decision to have a child—it's momentous. It is to decide forever to have your heart go walking around outside your body.

— Elizabeth Stone

Making the decision not to have a child—this is also momentous. It is a complicated choice, and, in my case, a choice borne of a host of reasons, fears, justifications and politics. It is not a choice made lightly; I am well aware that it will have repercussions throughout the span of my life. It is not a choice made without some feeling of regret, of loss. It is to decide forever to have my heart whispering—what if?

Physiologically, I am constructed so that I may incubate a fetus, or even a whole string of them, if I so choose. I will die one day, never having carried out the principal biological impetus for my being. Not for me the tender, nine-month bond between mother and child, the new life stirring in my belly, the poignancy of a tiny foot kicking at me from within. How does it feel to be connected so profoundly to another being? To share every waking and sleeping moment, every thought, every feeling, every cell? To sing and read sweet stories to my womb, and imagine that tiny creature inside, listening? These miracles I will never know.

But let's not be maudlin. There are advantages, definite perks, to this unpregnant state. Not for me the wrenching horrors of morning sickness, the swollen feet, the compressed and compromised bladder; not for me the agonizing hours of labour, the struggle of conscience over whether to submit to the welcome anaesthesia of the epidural, the always-unwelcome episiotomy. Ne'er shall I sport a T-shirt blaring "Baby Under Construction" or "Mommy in Training," nor will I wear the monstrously deformed maternity jeans. Never will I be expected to accept cheerfully the parade of strangers' hands caressing my ripe belly, hoping to extract a little of the magical force that burnishes even the most exhausted of expectant women with a preternatural glow. Caesarean section, postpartum depression, being heckled for breastfeeding in public—these too I shall never know, at least not first-hand.

We have all heard the argument that people who choose not to have children are selfish. This may be true, for certainly the child-free state facilitates self-indulgence: without children, I have the freedom to travel, to stay out late, to eat nothing but toast—or, better yet, cake—for dinner. I am not constantly required to set a good example; not expected to pass on the appropriate pleasantries and restraints required for high functioning in polite society—no farting, no belching, no elbows on the table. I will save money. Having children—feeding them, clothing them, entertaining them, educating them—can be fabulously expensive. Perhaps most significantly for me, being child-free has allowed me to explore life by taking on a series of temporary and often low-paying jobs, jobs frequently lacking benefits and opportunities for advancement, simply because I find them interesting. As a parent, it is unlikely that I would have this luxury; in order to provide security for my children, I would lock in to the best job I could find. Naturally, most parents are willing to make such sacrifices for their children—but that is not to say that parenthood does not also have its selfish side.

I often ask colleagues why they decided to have children, and their responses are not uniformly magnanimous. To carry on the family name. A chance to see the world with new eyes. Because I was lonely. Because I got pregnant. Because that's what people do. Rarely are my own fears echoed, though I can't imagine they are unconsidered: who will take care of me when I am old, if indeed I should require taking care of, as so many of us ultimately do? Who will I call when I am lonely, when my back goes out and I can't hoist myself off the couch, when I run out of groceries and my pension cheque is late? Who will remember me with the love due only to a mother; who will keep my photos, my letters, the other treasured mementoes of this life I have lived; and what but these will represent the sum total of my days on this Earth? What will remain of me, when I have gone, but that single withered branch on the family tree?

Having a child is to leave a legacy. Who wants to leave this world and be forgotten, when to be forgotten is to die completely? Who wants to take the chance of growing old and infirm and being utterly alone? Having children does not guarantee against this, of course, but it certainly reduces the probability. I love my nieces dearly, and they love me, I've no doubt. But when they are grown and have their own aging parents, their own families to consider, where will I fit in? My own family had an elderly aunt, in similar circumstances, who made great demands upon us. When I once told my grandma that I didn't want children of my own, she responded in horror, "You aren't going to be like Aunt Ethel?!"

I was taken aback. *Of course* I wouldn't be like Aunt Ethel! Would I? Had Aunt Ethel been "like Aunt Ethel" only because she did not have her own immediate family to take care of, to take care of her?

So I pondered the status of the child-free relative. It is subtle, but palpable, the reduced emphasis on those without children. There is some whiff of ambivalence, some ever-so-slight marginalization of the one who fails to procreate, to ensure the continuation of the familial DNA. To wit: no matter how much I am loved by the other members of my family, they do not come to see me. They will protest—"We visit you all the time!"—but they visit me only peripherally. I have lived on Vancouver Island for seven years; they live on the mainland. When my younger sister and her daughter moved to the Island four years ago, the rest of the family—not one of whom had come to the Island in the three years I'd been there—began visiting with regularity.

It's not that I mind, terribly; it's not that I don't understand; it's not that I cannot rationalize it to death; but there is the nagging reality that, on some level, one feels diminished. Think of the baby shower where the poor mother is sidelined as the guests exclaim over the frightened child with rabid glee; then imagine, behind the poor mother, the child-free sister, permanently sidelined.

The commonest fallacy among women is that simply having children makes one a mother, which is as absurd as believing that having a piano makes one a musician.
— Sydney J. Harris

When I was growing up, I never dreamed of marriage and children. I don't know why. Perhaps I was too preoccupied with reading, catching frogs and digging up bugs in the backyard. As I grew older, I never began dreaming of marriage and children. Sometimes I wondered at this—particularly since my older sister yearned for nothing more dearly than a family of her own. Years ago, introspective after the breakup of a relationship, I mused aloud, "I have never wanted to get married or have children, and you have never wanted anything more. Did Mom and Dad raise us so differently?"

She surprised me with her answer. "It's not what Mom and Dad did, it's you and me. When we were little, I was always sick. I needed you. You just don't want to be needed any more." My sister had a

chronic health condition for which she had frequently been hospitalized as a child. When she was home, she often relied on me to be her
nursemaid. I had never considered this to be a formative experience,
but the insight was illuminating and has since inspired me to examine
my relationship with my younger sister as well.

I was close to four and a half years old, and my older sister near-
ing eight, when our parents asked us if we would like a younger sister
or brother. I remember being somewhat blasé about it. I'm not sure
whether I became much more excited over the next few months, but I
do clearly recall sitting in the hallway of the hospital, silently, with my
father and older sister, surrounded by nauseating mint-green everything, waiting. Then walking out the door together, this new family
of five, all eyes on that tiny plump mysterious something swaddled in
white—or maybe pink—clutched to my mother's breast.

Well. I do know that my enthusiasm for that tiny plump mysterious something grew steeply once we got it home. There must be hundreds of pictures of me toting my baby sister around, grinning wildly.
Maybe I decided then that this was my baby, and I was determined to
take care of it. Her. I sang her to sleep. For years. When she was old
enough to get into trouble and be sent to her room, I would sneak in
to comfort her. Very probably I undermined a good deal of what little
disciplinary action she was subjected to. Recent musings on the topic
prompted my now-all-grown-up little sister to confide, "It was kind of
like having two mothers, but one was more sympathetic."

So, perhaps on some level I feel I have already fulfilled my
mothering duties, and it is time to direct my energies elsewhere. Perhaps I cannot imagine loving a child of my own any more than I love
my nieces, and the thought is daunting. Certainly, it is not that my
maternal instinct has dissipated. I love babies, I am gaga over toddlers and I worry constantly about stray animals, children at risk,
people without homes. My parents taught me to "put yourself in the

other person's shoes," and I never looked back. I am a seething mass of empathy; I can't listen to the news without being driven to tears for the plight of some stranger or other. There are so many sad stories, so many people in need, and I view human overpopulation as a large part of the problem. The planet is overrun with humanity. We are incapable of living together peaceably, of distributing resources to ensure that there is enough for each of us, of consistently treating each other and the Earth itself with respect. We waste, pollute and destroy at a ridiculous rate. By not having children, I am choosing not to contribute to this problem. I am choosing to leave more room for the children who are already here.

We have all heard the adage that it takes a village to raise a child. This is my parenting philosophy. I dream, not of having children of my own, but of parenting when and where and whom I can—as a sort of universal parent, a Mother at Large, if you will. I don't need to produce a child in order to mother; I can mother in a hundred different ways. I can love the children in my life. I can contribute to local associations that work to end violence against women and children; that provide food and shelter to people in need; that assist single-parent families. I can knit hats and buy warm clothes and blankets to donate to children in the winter. Through international aid organizations, I can support foster kids, fund schools and buy medical supplies for children I will never know. I can give change to panhandlers and buy meals for people on the street. I can help animal-rights organizations. I can and I do, all this and more. My parenting energy encompasses children of all ages, of all species.

I mother in a hundred little ways, every day. It isn't much, but it's what I do. Sometimes it's exhausting. As exhausting as "real" mothering? I'll never know. But this, I realize now, this is my role, this is who I am as a parent. If having a child does not automatically make one a mother, then not having a child cannot prohibit me from being one. My child-free status has not rendered me incapable of sustaining life; worthless for cultivation; unprofitable; empty. What of barrenness, then? If I am a vessel, I am full to overflowing with love and strength and the milk of human kindness. I have not borne a child, but I am a universal parent; in a hundred little ways my love can change the world.

Adrienne Munro was born and raised in Kamloops, B.C., but now lives in Victoria with her partner. She has a degree in archaeology and a diploma in cultural resources management. She has previously been published in *A Woman's Place: Art and the Role of Women in the Cultural Formation of Victoria, B.C., 1850s to 1920s*, edited by K.A. Finlay.

alien invasion

CANDACE FERTILE

A SUNDAY AFTERNOON, A FAMILY GATHERING. Cousins playing badminton on the front lawn. A crisis — my seven-year-old self has a tantrum, totally out of character, about my younger, pampered brother. If he gets another turn, I want one. Tears drown my face but cannot mask the roaring around me. I am having a tantrum and a panic attack simultaneously, but only the latter is familiar. The world recedes behind thick, watery glass, wavy and muffled by the din in my brain. Everyone is standing still, looking at me. I do not like to be the centre of attention. A voice pierces my painful frailty as a cousin whispers, with the horrible derision of a teenage girl, "Well, if this is what having children is like, I'm never going to have any."

I see my mother on the fringes of the lawn with other adults, looking shocked at my behaviour, but I am too stunned by my cousin's words to do anything but think, "I hope you never have kids. You just don't understand." I trail disconsolately off into the backyard to console myself with Buddy, a comforting Samoyed in whose fur I can bury my face.

That cousin eventually had children. I did not. Last night at dinner, a man asked if I regretted never having children. "No," I answered. "It was a relief to discover that I had a choice."

I never wanted to become a mother, but I assumed it was what I would do as that seemed to be the way of the world when I was growing up in the 1950s and '60s. Every woman I knew was a mother—my own mom, my aunts, my friends' mothers, neighbourhood moms and television moms. Occasionally teachers were single women, but they got married and disappeared into motherhood and domesticity. My girlfriends fantasized about their weddings and the names of their children. They developed crushes on boys and practised writing Mrs. So and So. I practised my own signature in case I became famous and people wanted my autograph. Should I do a beautiful lacy signature or opt for something indecipherable and speedy? Even with the somewhat embarrassing last name of "Fertile," I never imagined being someone else or someone's mother.

Why? No doubt the reasons are multiple. Or perhaps simple— maybe I am just missing that motherhood gene. But when I think about it, strong feelings surge over me.

✒ PREGNANCY

The idea gives me the creeps, the ultimate invasion of privacy by an alien. I dislike having people stand too close to me—you know, the ones at cocktail parties who keep inching forward while you back up until you smash into a wall, spilling precious drops of martini. I certainly don't want some whole strange person curled up inside me, snoozing and feeding at will. The alien inside can make women desire unlikely combinations of food (pickles and ice cream being the stereotype, and I loathe pickles). No wonder some women puke until they have nothing left inside them except this demanding creature who pushes and shoves his or her way around the womb, and then, when it's time to face the world, frequently resists (who wouldn't?) being expelled into a hostile environment, creating unspeakable pain (no, I never bought the "It's just a little discomfort" view).

The alien inside discombobulates hormones and affects all manner of behaviour apart from eating—one of the most important being sleep. I love sleeping. I frequently wake up in the morning or whatever time I wake and think, "Rats, I'm awake." Allowing an alien the power to disturb an essential part of life is unthinkable. The alien inside changes a woman's body forever. Forget the breathtakingly beautiful Demi Moore on the cover of *Vanity Fair* wearing nothing but her skin and toting that interior alien. Forget those so-called "yummy mummies" who pop out aliens and spring back into their size zero (mental note—we'll soon be in negative numbers for clothing sizes) designer duds, handing off their aliens to—hmmm, often more aliens, resident aliens that is—poor women who have to leave their own children to care for the spawn of the pampered rich. No: those fetal aliens generally cause swollen bodies, blotchy skin and crankiness in women. And the crankiness has to escalate when the exhausted vessel does not snap back into the perfect shape it never was.

I recall the hormonal deluge that enabled a pregnant friend to consume an entire pan of Nanaimo bars in one sitting. In the time it took for me to give her the recipe over the phone and take the bus to the other side of the river, where she was staying with the older and miraculously sympathetic sister of a friend of ours, she had scarfed down several thousand calories. If being pregnant could make someone do that, I thought, the state really is perilous.

BABIES

They are needy. It's their job. They need it all—food, clothing, bathing, attention, diapers, love, baby flashcards, space-age strollers, odd flowery headbands or ball caps, Baby on Board signs, Michelin tires and BabyGap. Or someone thinks they need these things. Babies cannot tell us specifically what they need. They have to make noise. Lots of noise. Loud noise. Noise that causes the cat to run away from home.

Noise that makes the dog look dolefully at its competition and realize the contest was fixed from the beginning. Need is the essence of babies. They have no choice. They need to be breastfed, but they frequently do not master this new skill quickly. After all, they just came from a place where they lounged about while all needs for survival were provided. So they may not suck contentedly at their mother's breast (which is often cracked and bleeding from the attempts to meet the baby's nutritional requirements).

They need to have their diapers changed. Baby boys pee in their unwitting parents' faces. Now a device called a "teepee" is available, a cone one places over the baby's penis to prevent impromptu showers. Diaper changing demands first of all choosing the diapers—cloth or disposable, both of which have drawbacks and ecological side effects. And baby pee and poop are still urine and excrement. Nevertheless, what comes out of a baby results in meticulous examination by parents, and much discussion. Sometimes it even results in reporting the findings to child-free friends.

Babies need attention. Of course, they do—they can't do much, so other people have to take up the slack. But do they need baby talk? What's wrong with the regular vernacular, whatever it is? And if babies do require baby talk (I like to keep an open mind on communication), child-free friends don't. Privacy addicts such as I do not need to know the pet names lovers have for their partners' fun parts. Nor do we need to passively participate in the dumbing down of the language.

Babies need care—the warmth, the love, the affection, the basic needs met, the whole welcome-to-the-world thing that all human beings should experience. But not everyone wants to provide specific moments of baby care. Please do not thrust your precious bundle upon me as if you are doing me a huge favour. Thrust a martini (vodka, shaken, olives) upon me while I gaze at your child and make polite positive comments. Do not offer to "let" me babysit. From age 11 to 13, I babysat children because their parents paid me. Now I have a different job. I teach at a college and, while small aspects of babysitting sneak in, I get paid more. Much more. And tussle with no diapers.

The things I do not understand about what babies need include Baby on Board signs. We are supposed to be more careful drivers because there's a baby in the car? But nine-year-olds and grandparents don't matter? I understand the monetary impetus for Michelin tire advertisements, but they are a cheap shot at parents who cannot afford such consumer goods or make other choices. Babies are important. But they should not be used as advertising gimmicks. At least adults make a choice about appearing in stupid ads.

Baby getups also concern me. Baby pierced ears, for example. I had to wait until I was 16 to get my ears pierced (life was tougher in the Dark Ages), and it hurt. But I got to choose. Babies have always reflected the status of their parents, but now the consumer society has made babies a fashion and "lifestyle" accessory instead of small human beings requiring care. Is a baby in a brand-new designer outfit better off than one in hand-me-downs? Has a baby ever worn out a piece of clothing? Does a baby care about a logo on a T-shirt?

TODDLERS

They too are needy. See above, except add the fact that they can move faster than babies and therefore find more ways to hurt themselves in their experimentation with the world. They need extreme vigilance, and I know I would forget about the toddler and all the life-threatening stuff in the house while I was deep into the life-threatening stuff in Henry James' *Portrait of a Lady* or Louise Erdrich's *Love Medicine* or Guy Vanderhaeghe's *The Englishman's Boy* or Carol Shields' *The Stone Diaries* or any other book I was reading. I have selective hearing. When I read, I hear the voices of the book. Mothers have told me that I would not behave this way if I had children, but the risk is too great, as I do think children are important. But the main reason is that I would rather imagine than experience small children. In a way, my desire, even need, to read is as great as someone's desire or need to have a child. I marvel at women who can do both, but again, many mothers have told me that they don't do both—reading for several hours a day is not compatible with caring for small children.

ADOLESCENTS AND TEENAGERS

Older children are needy. See above and add hormonal changes, driving, drugs and peer pressure. I was a teenager decades ago with all those factors slamming at my sense of self. It was, to put it mildly, an unpleasant time. I did not like going through it, and I do not wish to endure it through the experience of a child I am responsible for. At 16, one of my best friends got pregnant. Such events in a good Catholic family were rewarded with shunning. The baby (my now-35-year-old goddaughter) was two years old before my friend's parents spoke to her. The whole situation scared the crap out of me. However, as a geek, I had minimal luck getting dates, let alone fumbling with bigger sexual issues.

My own experiences driving make me realize I would stay awake forever (and that sleep deprivation would be dangerous on a global scale) if a child of mine were out behind the wheel. Managing to roll a Volvo station wagon when I was 14 (the age for a learner's permit in Alberta back then in the aforesaid Dark Ages) is one of my less impressive feats. That car survived both me and my brother, who used to pretend it was an off-road vehicle. Both of us are extraordinarily lucky we did not hurt anyone. And luck is all it was.

I have no idea if drugs are worse today than when I was a teenager. I suspect they are, and I see the heartache of parents with children involved in substance abuse. The thought of such pain is unendurable to me. Once again luck enters the picture—I do not have an addictive personality, if one eliminates books (which can after all be obtained free at a public library), shoes, cashmere sweaters and travel. These things do not kill or maim anything but a credit card.

2 When I was young and thought that having children was just part of the program, I imagined putting my son or daughter in a Styrofoam suit before release into the wild. I knew ultimate protection was impossible. I also knew the crazy things kids do. I didn't want to be responsible. I chose not to be responsible for another human being, other than in the larger sense of trying to be a decent person. With relatively safe birth-control methods, I could exercise the choice.

Or is it a choice? Maybe the space for the "mommy" gene is taken up with the "reader-traveller" gene. Maybe the words of my father—"Anyone can get married and have children, but you can do something more important"—nested in my brain and gave birth to the no-birth clause. Maybe the words of my mother—"Getting married and having children ruins your life"—tainted the whole experience for me. I know the heartfelt meanness of my cousin that day on the front lawn will never leave me and had an effect on how I view motherhood. I am an adult and have been for decades. Our experiences as children in our own families and communities help shape us. But are we under complete mind-control (movies and the CIA notwithstanding)? Nope. We make choices and live with the consequences. Even in the absence of choice, we must live with the consequences of actions.

Motherhood is a threshold that, once crossed, cannot be eradicated, and there are some journeys I do not wish to make. Ironically, it's like death—"the bourn from which no traveller returns" as Hamlet says. In becoming a mother, a woman goes to a new place, I think, and I never wanted to go to a place that I could not come home from. Home, for me, is a serene, alien-free place of repose and reading, the place I return to after I step out into the world, whether it's to go to work or visit friends (and their children) or explore new landscapes and cultures. The country and culture of motherhood are gained only as a one-way trip, and I have always bought return tickets.

Candace Fertile has a Ph.D. in English from the University of Alberta and teaches at Camosun College in Victoria, B.C. She traces her Metis roots back to her Cree grandmother. She is a regular book reviewer for numerous publications, including *The Globe and Mail*, *The Edmonton Journal* and *The Vancouver Sun*. She is also the poetry editor for *Room of One's Own*.

life outside
the plan

MAGGIE DE VRIES

BY THE TIME I WAS 27, I WOULD BE MARRIED with two children, a girl and a boy, born in that order, two years apart. I would be a teacher, I thought, perhaps at home for a few years until the children were schoolaged. Maybe I would do some writing as well. That was my plan. Those were my interests.

Then I grew up. Life didn't fit tidily into my plan or my plan didn't fit tidily into my life. First of all, there was the husband to come up with. Once I hit my 20s and university, a husband was the furthest thing from my mind.

When I was 28 (none of my childhood plans realized), I moved back to Vancouver, after years away, to do my master's degree in English literature at the University of British Columbia. I had been living in Guelph, Ontario, for two years. A close friend of mine, Amanda, and her husband were both moving to Vancouver as well, to begin Ph.D.s Amanda and I drove across the country in her enormous, ancient, beat-up car. We turned the back seat into a big bed for Noah and Araba, her two small children who travelled with us. Her husband and her older daughter, Ya-Asantwa, made the journey separately.

I settled into my mother's basement and into the English department and back into old friendships. That Christmas, two friends from Montreal, Jenny and Dan, came to stay with me with their four-month-old baby. On December 22, we were having breakfast and making plans to borrow Mum's car and go for a drive to the North Shore when Mum called me upstairs. St. Paul's Hospital had just called to tell her that her daughter was in labour. It couldn't be me. It had to be Sarah. I stood there, frozen, stunned. Sarah was my sister, eight years younger. She was 21 that Christmas, and she had been living downtown, supporting herself by selling sex, for four years steadily and for seven years on and off. Over the years she had developed a serious heroin habit. Life was a terrible struggle for her. And we had had no idea that she was pregnant. My mother set off for the hospital, and I made my way back downstairs, sobbing.

It was hard for Jenny to understand why I was so upset about a new baby, but I was. We continued with some version of our plans, but I was not mentally present. Later that day, Mum phoned to tell us that Sarah had given birth to a healthy baby girl. The next day I visited mother and daughter.

Three weeks later I was pregnant.

Well, I didn't know it at the time, of course. The father was from the United States, in Vancouver to celebrate New Year's Eve the night we met, and to attend an Alice in Chains concert two weeks later (yes, slam-dancing and all; I remember having sore toes the next day). We connected, enjoyed each other's company, but not deeply. Later, we went camping together and sailing. He supported me as best he could when I told him that I was pregnant. I can only imagine how profound his relief was when I followed that statement up instantly with my plan to have an abortion.

That decision had not been easy. My period, always predictable, had not come on schedule, and I had waited for it in silence, day after day, certainty mounting. It was about 10 days late, I think, when I went with some friends to stay for the weekend on Galiano Island. We all spread out our sleeping bags in a big loft area of the house. I remember telling a close friend that I thought I might be pregnant. I was fairly calm about it, or appeared to be. At the time, I was fantasizing about keeping the child, imagining what that would be like. The idea had some appeal, but it was hard to see how I could fit a child into my life, without a partner, living in my mother's basement, still in graduate school. And I felt that children deserved access to both their parents, yet I could not imagine involving the father of this child in our lives. The thought horrified me.

I had always believed that women had the right to choose abortion, but I also knew instinctively that it was not a decision to be taken lightly. A fetus was growing in my body. If I left things as they were, I would almost certainly have a baby. An abortion would destroy that life, however one defined it. My mother told me that she would help me if I chose to have the baby, that I could stay at home for as long as I needed to. She must have been stunned to be raising one daughter's baby and then find herself faced with the possibility of a second grandchild in the house. If she was, though, she did not show it. A friend of my mother's impressed upon me the seriousness of my decision. Abortions leave wounds behind, she said. Loss. Grief.

I had lunch with Amanda, mother of four, and asked for her insight. She told me that my pregnancy was an expression of love, my body responding to my niece's presence in my life. Whether I had an abortion or not, she said, that love would flow into people's lives, into my niece's life. I know that I am not remembering her words correctly, but I took with them a powerful message of her love for me and her support for me in whatever decision I made. Such support from a woman who had had four babies, who knew in every cell of her body what pregnancy leads to, what it means, was deeply significant. She wasn't telling me what to do; she was telling me that whatever I did do, it would be all right. It would be right for me. When Amanda died of breast cancer in 1998 at the age of 37, the loss was terrible for all of us.

In the end, I met with the doctor, went back a few days later to the day clinic, put on the robe and booties, lay down on the bed. I remember being wheeled through the hall, the administration of the anaesthetic and waking up in the recovery room, lying on my side. When were they going to do it? I wondered. Then I realized that they already had. I started to cry. A nurse checked on me and gave me a tissue.

And that was my abortion. I still feel sad about it sometimes. I figure out how old the child would be. I try to imagine my life with a teenager in it. I try to comprehend what it means to have done what I did. I regret that I got pregnant when I wasn't ready to, but despite the moral complexity of abortion, despite my own pain around it and despite the fact that I have not had a child, I do not regret ending the pregnancy.

Eighteen months later, I met my future husband. I had told myself that having a child later on would somehow balance giving up a child in my late 20s. When I met Roland and our relationship grew serious, I assumed that eventually we would marry and have children. Then one night we were talking in bed, and Roland told me that he never wanted to have children. I rolled away from him and wept. I considered getting out of the bed, dressing and going home, ending the relationship then and there. But I did not.

Over the next year, we talked about children a great deal. I thought that if Roland just realized how much they would enrich his life, he would change his mind. I thought that he was afraid. I thought that he didn't know what was best for him. (And I, of course, did.)

No matter how much we talked, we resolved nothing. He did not want children. I did. He was committed to my niece, Jeanie. If anything happened to my mother, we would become Jeanie's guardians.

But he was not willing to bring his own child into the world. At last it started to sink in. Roland did not want children. It wasn't that he didn't know his own mind and heart. It wasn't that he was afraid of the responsibility. It wasn't that he wasn't experienced with children and didn't know what he was missing. He actually knew his own mind. I started to ease up on the endless conversations on the topic.

We wanted to get married, but this important issue remained unresolved. At last, in the fall of 1994, we decided that we wanted to be together more than we wanted to get our own way on the child question. We wanted to do what was best for us together rather than for either of us individually. We were willing to seek counselling later on if we felt that we needed help in making up our minds. On July 29, 1995, we married. I was just short of 34 years old.

I think that the combination of my realization that Roland knew what he wanted, our agreement that we would do what was best for us together and the passage of time are the elements that finally settled the issue. I have had a group of four close women friends since elementary school. With their partners and Roland, we now make a group of nine. Although none of us had made the firm decision not to have children, we passed from our 30s into our 40s four years ago, all childless. In a way, time got the better of us. One couple in our group has now adopted two little girls, but still, we have all gone through most of the last 15 years with no pressure from our closest friends to have children; the culture of our group has remained predominantly adult. Most of us are blessed with nieces and nephews, we women have embraced the role of aunt, and now we have the one couple's daughters to enjoy. Perhaps I should speak only for myself when I say that I have come to enjoy the freedom that comes without children. And I enjoy the children in my life that much more with such freedom.

One of the most important adults in my life when I was a little girl was my aunt, the children's author, Jean Little. She had no children of her own, and she devoted a great deal of energy to her nieces and nephews. I loved my aunts who were mothers as well, of course, but an aunt without children was able to give something extra special to me.

I hope I can be an aunt like that.

I am, as it turns out, nobody's mother, and I am sad to miss out on that experience. But there are many ways to replenish the Earth and there are many ways to live a full life. In the last three or four years, I have felt, for the first time in my life, that I am on the right path for me. I look forward to seeing where it leads.

Maggie de Vries is the author of *Missing Sarah*, a memoir about her sister, one of the women who was killed while living on the Downtown Eastside in Vancouver. She is an editor at Orca Books and the author of several children's books. In 2005, she finished a stint as author-in-residence at the Vancouver Public Library. She continues to enjoy her life as a wife, friend, writer, editor and community activist.

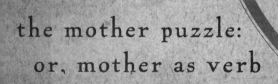

the mother puzzle:
or, mother as verb

KATE BRAID

For Kevin Steeves

I have two children. I have five.
I have no children.
I have one child, a dozen. I had two before I was six.
I have no children.
I raised a son.

THE TRIP FROM NANAIMO to Vancouver on a British Columbia ferry is more peaceful than any highway. A few weeks ago, I chose a comfortable chair on the north side of the ship and settled in to enjoy the calm of water, mountains and sky when two teens dropped into the seats beside me, looking ridiculously young for their cargo. Each carried a new baby, and they proceeded to talk, non-stop, about babies: baby soothers, baby teeth, baby colic.

It was obvious by the way they frequently glanced in my direction, eager and smiling, eyebrows raised as if to say, "Isn't this exciting?" that they wanted me to join the conversation.

I frowned out the window. I sank deeper into my chair. I hoisted a newspaper. Eventually they got up and moved to some other part of the ship where there was, perhaps, a more appreciative audience, while I was left to wonder why I'd been so curmudgeonly.

℘ I've never borne my own children, but from the time I was two there was a string of new babies in our house—five of them. Our mother was well organized; we all had our jobs and mine was "the kids." I fed them, dressed them, put them to bed and minded them when Mum was out or busy. In our home movies, I am the one looking righteous, upright and preternaturally organized, watching the younger ones. In my 13-year-old mind I figured I'd raised them all, especially the two babies.

My father was a businessman. In the 1950s, that explained everything: why he was never home for dinner, why he drank so much. The household hinged on him: he seemed to get everything his way; every activity was based on his agenda; he won every argument. When I was 12 and asked my mother why, she said, "Someone has to give in."

"But why is it always you?"

A few months later, when my girlfriends start talking about marriage and babies as if these are givens, my mouth opens to say, "I'm never getting married. I'm never having kids." I know this isn't what I'm supposed to say, that all girls should want babies, but I don't. I've already raised two babies, five. I want something else, something different.

℘ It isn't until I'm 30 that I find what that "something" is.

I'd been living on one of the Gulf Islands and had run out of money. Out of desperation, I stumbled into a job as a construction labourer. The year was 1977.

One of my first jobs was to help pour concrete for a new basement. While the carpenters ran wheelbarrows along raised ramps, and dumped the wet mud between the formed walls like Jell-O into a mould, my task was to brace a wooden chute directly in front of where they were pouring, so the thick liquid was directed downward into the walls instead of shooting over the top. I braced my shoulder, my entire body, behind the chute as the men tipped wheelbarrow after wheelbarrow, and the powerful soup of cement, gravel, water and sand thundered inches from my head into the forms.

"It's setting up! Hurry! The chute!"

I had never been part of anything so intense, so physical, so exhilarating, in my life.

Two days later we were back to strip the walls.

After we'd knocked down the bracing, Ted, the carpenter I was working with, laid his hands on the top board of the wall nearest him and gave a violent heave. It hesitated, then surrendered with a slight suck and a snap—and there was the wall. It was concrete, yes, but not the dull stuff of sidewalks. This was a grey sculpture embossed with every ring and ripple and knot of the shiplap that had formed it—and I had been a part of creating this thing of lasting and useful beauty.

There was no one to talk to about my delight in construction—in concrete—and the men only laughed. So I began keeping notes, talking to myself.

Mother · *verb* 1 give birth to **2** protect as a mother.

—Canadian Oxford Dictionary

Other people oohed and aahed, but I found babies, well, boring. They couldn't talk. I had some wonderful moments with nieces and nephews, building forts and sharing Christmas, but then I was happy to go home. Always, I'd rather be reading, which is what I did, as much and as often as I possibly could, oblivious to everything except the black letters on a white page in front of my eyes, wildly alive in my imagination. People said, "Your own will be different," but I didn't care to test that truth. So it was a bit of a surprise that when I got pregnant, my first response was delight.

✒ I was 24, living with a man with whom I felt happy and cared for, when we went for a holiday to Banff where, in a motel beside the Bow River, we made love. I knew I was pregnant the moment it happened.

"How could you know that?" he asked, without waiting for an answer, but I was certain.

This was 1971, an exhilarating time when women had both the birth-control pill and, now, access to therapeutic (meaning legal, safe and in a hospital under a doctor's care) abortions. Now we could choose our lovers, choose our pregnancies.

But we underestimated the weight of choice.

When the doctor confirmed I was pregnant, I was ecstatic. I forgot about raising babies when I was 13, forgot my vow of no children.

"I'm pregnant!" I announced as I came in the front door. We'd have a baby, we'd convert the television room, we'd teach it how to swim ....

"You'll have an abortion, of course," my partner said. The words were like a rock in my face.

"Of course," I said.

I felt stricken. But I was too young, too unsure of myself to argue with him. He was older; he must know better. I had an abortion.

Afterwards, I was numb. I understood slowly that, just as in my father's house, here too, there was an agenda—my boyfriend's. That it was not to be discussed. That having a baby would disturb it and that he didn't want to share me with a child. Of course, I thought. And certainly I'd never wanted a child; it was just that we hadn't even talked about it.

Two years later we broke up because I realized again—as we struggled to form a commune—that there was an agenda there too. I was not to be consulted because it was assumed I would go along. But this time, I wasn't willing. Instead, I would go back to school, move to an island, stumble upon the joys of construction and a career that took all my passion and energy. There was no room for a child in my life. I got a dog.

The second time I got pregnant, I was single, still living on the island, working in construction. I loved building things, working outdoors, feeling my body fit and lean and powerful, making the best money I'd ever made. So why did so many people—men and women—feel so uncomfortable about what I was doing? How should I reply to the sheet-metal worker who said flatly, "Women shouldn't be doing this." If construction was "men's" work, as they claimed, what did that make me?

I loved the work with such a passion, I decided I'd ignore the people who found me difficult to classify. I'd defy anyone who tried to pigeonhole me, do exactly what I wanted to do. When I got pregnant again, again I knew precisely who and when, but the man refused to believe the child was his.

This time, I wanted it. Well, not exactly "wanted." Not exactly "I." It was my body that wanted, or—I was 31—perhaps it was purely hormones. Perhaps it was those voices whispering behind me all my life: "Do as we expect. Have babies. Settle down. Last chance."

My mind was busy. I was taking university courses long-distance, finishing a master's degree, learning construction skills, gaining confidence, thinking of becoming a carpenter one day, while my body demanded, screamed, insisted on a baby. Every cell in me wanted it while all my rational senses said it wasn't right: I had no steady job, no profession, no skills, no money, no desire for a child. Further, the father wouldn't acknowledge it. I decided, finally, on an abortion. I went to the city and told my very pregnant gynecologist what I'd decided, but as she got up to see me to the door my hand brushed her belly and I felt the firmness of the baby inside her—and changed my mind. "I'll call you!" I cried over my shoulder.

Every day counted. No decision was also a decision, and I didn't want to decide by default. I wanted to choose my life, live by my own agenda. But I felt paralyzed. All my resources, my intelligence, my friends, my books—nothing gave me a clear answer.

On Solstice Eve, I went to a community dance in a grassy field under a full moon. My friends were there, dancing to a Celtic band playing fierce reels, but I could hardly concentrate on the music. I was lost. Every question led to a different answer. So I gave up. I stopped trying. I only danced. I hid in the music, in a field, under a full moon, mindless, until tears began to stream down my face and I knew I had decided again, or it was decided, and this time for the final time.

I accepted then, as I had not before, that as I walked into the gynecologist's office again, there was sadness but not regret.

My mother offered to fly across the country from Montreal to be with me. I was grateful for the acceptance implied in her offer but I was also afraid; what if she deep-down disapproved? Women were supposed to want their babies, weren't they? Afterwards, I was sorry I'd told her "No." Sometimes, in breaking new ground, I've forgotten there can be comfort in the old.

℘ The following year I met a man I'd dated for several weeks before we spent our first night together in his communal house. In the morning as I came downstairs, two of the household's children raced through the hall below.

"Kate," John said. "I'd like you to meet my son, Kevin."

The boy stopped, looked up, a stoutly built blond child with dark brown eyes and a sweet face. He looked 12 though I later learned he was only seven.

"Hi," I said. Had I known John had a son or had I forgotten it in the rush of love?

Kevin stood very still—the girl had raced ahead of him out the door—and regarded me with solemn brown eyes.

"Here we go," he said.

Four months later, the three of us moved into our own rented house, and I became, officially, a stepmother.

I wasn't entirely sure about having a son. I mean, stepson. At least he was seven years old, an already-talking human being. But how should I do this? I didn't know any other step-parents, and when I scoured libraries I found only one book on step-parenting—a book of fiction. I tried to remember what it was like to mother my siblings but I had only been "sister," didn't know "mother" or "stepmother."

Kevin and I approached each other cautiously. He called me by my name, "Kate." I wasn't his mother; he already had a mother who lived only blocks away, whom he'd see every second weekend. What was I? And what should I call her, his "real" mother?

He was a polite, thoughtful child. When I asked him to do things, he did them. I was a polite adult. I tried to treat him with respect. Occasionally, especially at the beginning, I was jealous of the time John spent with Kevin, while I also felt deeply moved by a man who helped his son make Roman shields, who got up in the night to change sheets and put his son back to bed. I might not know how to be a mother, but John was clearly a father.

Mostly I stepped back. I let Kevin's dad and his birth mum make the big decisions in his life. After all, he was *their* son, wasn't he? Wasn't he?

In a way, it was a relief. I hadn't wanted my own babies, but here I had inherited one for whom I had only partial responsibility. Still, he lived with us, and I had to find a way to be with him. I did know there were some things, a tone of voice my own mother had used, that I hated. We kids had called it The Mother Voice.

One day when I was angry at Kevin for some small thing—racing through the house, perhaps—I snapped at him in the exact tone my mother had used on me. It was The Mother Voice I had sworn I would never, ever, use with my child (if I ever had one, which I wouldn't). I halted in mid-sentence. Kevin, too, froze. As we faced each other, a decision was made. I took a deep breath. As if he understood the new pact between us, Kevin stepped quietly past me, out of the kitchen, back to his friends. We would do it another way. I was grateful, and slightly in awe of what seemed the innate wisdom of the child, his grace.

℘ Mother • *noun* **1a** a woman in relation to a child or children to whom she has given birth. **1b** a woman who serves as a mother, e.g., a step-mother, adoptive mother, or foster mother.

I remember once when my mother and father had gone out for the evening, leaving us with a babysitter. I'd been sick and my mother promised she'd come check on me. I woke out of a deep, fevered sleep to feel the warmth of her bent over me. She was dressed in her special going-out dress, wearing the glittering borealis beads that are now mine, and I could smell her best perfume. The room was dark, lit only by the light shining in from the hall. She leaned down, kissed me and said, "Do you mind if your father and I stay out a little longer?" and I answered out of the dream, without thinking, "Don't go."

Immediately I saw the regret in her eyes and was sorry. She rarely got a chance to socialize and I knew, in the unspoken way that children know, how much she missed dressing up and putting on her makeup and going out.

"It's okay," I said, trying to take it back.

But she'd seen my child's need and said, "I'll stay," with sadness, and I was selfishly glad.

I remember only that one time, but I know there must have been others. How many others? Times six kids?

My mother was the rudder and sail of our family ship. My father was the absentee owner who worked very hard, who paid the bills and came on board for the big occasions, but it was out of our mother's body that we six came, and in her care that we prospered. The belly of the boat. And that, I thought, is what a good mother does. She stays home with her sick kid instead of going to the party she yearns for.

She gives up the dress the man has given her money for, to buy shoes for one of the kids, eyeglasses for another.

I didn't want children of my own because I didn't believe I was capable of such sacrifice. I wasn't willing. I'd rather read.

⚘ In Grade 4, Kevin, a tall, heavy kid looking several years older than he actually was, often got picked on by older boys with a need to prove something by beating up the big kid. In those days, John's job often called him out of town, and it was while he was on one of those trips that Kevin came home with a note from his teacher saying he'd been disciplined—again—for fighting, and parental action was expected.

Parental action? I cleared my throat, said something inane like, "You know you shouldn't fight."

Kevin furrowed his brow and straightforwardly—as if explaining something difficult, which it was—said, "Kate, some things a boy just has to do."

It was his wisdom speaking. He did what had to be done. Of course. Some things a stepmother just has to accept. So I did.

Kevin was teaching me how to mother him, generous in giving me time to figure out a role that fit me, fit us, giving me time to come to love him, to name him my chosen child.

⚘ The notes I'd taken during my first construction job had become a book of poems. After my second book was published, I began to recognize a pattern: the long labour, the exultation of a newly emerging manuscript, then the blues that hit after its publication. I told a friend, "I don't have babies. I have books."

⚘ When I was 40 my closest friend, Jude, desperately wanted a child, but her partner did not. If she insisted, he would agree to be the father but then he would leave.

In the tradition of feminism, of the consciousness-raising groups we'd been in many times together over the years, Jude called a meeting of women friends. She chose carefully: one of us who'd always wanted children and had two of her own; two who'd had a single child late in life; a woman who'd chosen to have no children; and me, a stepparent. We sat in a circle holding hands and telling our stories, the why of what we'd decided, as if the "why" mattered, telling each other—more importantly—the consequence of our decisions.

When Jude decided, she had a girl, Sasha, and her partner stayed after all, a committed father. I was given the gift of being present at the birth and of being invited to become the godmother. Now I had a new child in my life, a baby.

℘ What does a godmother do? She visits the new mother on the second day after the birth and reads out loud the manual on breastfeeding while the mother groans and hangs her aching breasts over a bowl of hot water. A godmother who loves Shakespeare takes her goddaughter, age nine, to her first play, *A Midsummer Night's Dream*, and on the way home they "talk Shakespeare" at the child's request because she has heard iambic pentameter and it is music to her, as it is to the godmother. A godmother loves, and admires; she knits mod scarves and phones up to congratulate when things go well and add her comfort when they don't. A godmother, by then, has practised.

℘ **Mother** · *adjective* characteristic of a mother (*mother love*).

After 13 years in construction, I began teaching, first carpentry, then creative writing. A teacher has many roles. So when a student struggles with ornate and rambling poetry, then writes a poem about child rape that is clearly autobiographical—powerful, clear and gut-wrenching—and follows it with more, and when one year later she races into my office, takes my hand and leads me to the art gallery where she has an exhibit of those poems with paintings to illustrate them, then I feel like a mother, proud to see one of her offspring fly.

Mother figure • ***noun*** an older woman who is regarded as a source of nurture, support, etc.

I am lucky to have been born into a time and place when as a woman I had so many more choices than my own mother, or her mother. That day on the ferry, hearing the young women talk about babies was a reminder, and my curmudgeonly behaviour was a small shiver of grief at the inevitable cost. I chose not to have babies, but I had the good luck to find a stepson, a goddaughter, students, nephews and nieces, to be able to mother—the verb. For this, I am fiercely glad. There's more than one meaning to the word "mother," more than one way.

All the above is true.
I never wanted children.
This is less true.

Kate Braid was born in Alberta, raised in Montreal, went to school in New Brunswick and now lives in B.C. She had a checkered career as secretary, receptionist, teacher's aide and lumber piler until she "settled" as a carpenter for 15 years. She's on a one-year leave from teaching creative writing at Malaspina University-College to be Ruth Wynn Woodward Professor in Women's Studies at Simon Fraser University. She considers herself blessed to be surrounded by young people. Her books include *Inward to the Bones: Georgia O'Keeffe's Journey with Emily Carr; To This Cedar Fountain; Red Bait! Struggles of a Mine Mill Local,* with Al King; and *Covering Rough Ground,* which won the Pat Lowther Award.

afterword,
afterwards

LYNNE VAN LUVEN

THIS WEEK, AN ORDINARY WORK WEEK, two important things happened: my partner Andrew and I got a Valentine's card in the mail from Fort Qu'Appelle, Saskatchewan. It was handmade by my mother and my youngest nephew, Taitt, whom she babysits several afternoons a week. The card is made of pink construction paper and a round white paper doily which is centred with a deeper pink heart. "Be My Valentine," my mother has printed in pencil, in block letters, around the doily. Inside, on a folded sheet of paper, my mother writes in her cramped, spidery hand that my youngest sister, Michelle (21 years younger than me), is expecting her third child. A day later, an envelope arrived from Red Deer, Alberta. Inside, I find a picture of Jaxton Keats Kalenchuk, 6 pounds, 8 ounces, 20½ inches long. In the photo, my first great-nephew is just a few days old; he nestles on a sheepskin in a wicker basket, his eyes closed in inscrutable concentration. He wears a white-and-blue striped sleeper, the sleeves rolled up at the wrists. His legs are stretched out, tiny rosebud toes point straight toward the ceiling. He clasps two fingers of his right hand thoughtfully in his left. I study him, long and hard. Who is he waiting to become, this little sleeping soul? Once again, a whole new life has entered our clan, another tender shoot on the family tree.

I come from a largeish family with a fairly complex history. The new baby is my oldest niece Leah's first child; and Leah is my oldest brother's first child. Last summer, when we went to Fort Qu'Appelle for the wedding of my youngest niece, Regan, we met for the first time my middle niece Kelly's first baby daughter, Karyss, who looks exactly like her mother did as a baby. She is my parents' first great-grandchild and my first great-niece.

A day ago on the telephone, my middle sister, Colleen, (two sons, Landon and Carson) tells me that our sister Michelle's and our niece Regan's babies will both be born about the same time in June. I try to get my head around the fact that babies from two separate generations will be each other's close playmates. I have four siblings, all of whom have children, and now their children are having babies. Natural progression, family renewal. At the moment, my parents have 10 grandchildren and 2 great-grandchildren, with more of each in the offing. It's getting harder and harder for old Auntie Lynne to keep track.

A fecund lot, these Van Luven offspring. Except for me, of course, except for me.

🎜 Don't think for a moment that I wasn't like other little girls. I was, slavishly so. I played house, had an entourage of dolls, made mud pies, loved dresses with fluffy skirts. For the first five years of my life, I'm told, a crop of blond curls crowned my chubby little face. In junior high, I had crushes on my male teachers and agonized about the way my body was sprouting breasts and hips. In high school, I worried about my grades, my clothes and my figure, and was terrified about "going all the way." In many respects, I was your quintessential girly-girl. And I was more bookish than adventuresome.

My parents married at 19 (how young and vulnerable they look in their wedding pictures), and I was born a year later. As the first-born, I was the focus of my parents' and grandparents' attention—and the litmus of everyone's expectations. Then, four years after my birth, my brother Raymond came along, and my father's allegiances visibly shifted. Or so I felt.

I grew up on a small, mixed farm a few kilometres north of the Fort Qu'Appelle Valley, which, for those of you who have never left the Trans-Canada as you drive through Saskatchewan, is 60 miles north of Regina, Queen City of the Plains, formerly called Pile of Bones by the First Nations people. Because our farm was small and struggling, everything came down to production, and everyone had to help out. My mother was responsible for milking the cows, raising the chickens, slopping the hogs and planting and hoeing what seemed like acres of garden. We sold cream from the cows, sometimes eggs. My mother and I canned produce like mad every summer, the kitchen a steamy inferno, our nerves frazzled as we worked to put up garden-fresh corn, beans and tomatoes, as well as the rare case of store-bought peaches or cherries.

Everything had to earn its keep on our farm. If a hen stopped laying, she was butchered. If a cow became too old to calve, she was sent to market. If a dog, even a beloved pet, began to chase chickens or eat eggs, it was summarily shot. Every day, there was more work to be done than all of us could manage to complete, especially in the summer, when farming is a dawn-to-dusk proposition. Unlike other kids, I mostly dreaded summer holidays. Summer meant starting awake to a litany of chores running through my head.

And in July, it meant helping with the haying: wrestling bales of hay that were liberally spliced with thistles. In those primitive days, the small, square bales were stacked into pyramids that would eventually be collected in a tractor-drawn wagon and taken home to be stacked again in the barnyard, to be used as feed for the cattle over the winter.

I often joke that I became a feminist at 12 because I wasn't allowed to drive the tractor. Here's the crucial scene: a scorching July day. I'm a moody brooder, hoping my life will miraculously improve in August when I turn 13. I've already begun to fulminate about the injustices I see around me: the relentlessness of farm women's chores; the casual, unexamined misogyny passed from father to son; the way my mother scrimps, using her cream-cheque money to finance new kitchen curtains. As I hover around the kitchen, I find the women's talk depressing, especially when it dawns on me that very few farm wives are paid wages for their work, that most of them have to ask their husbands for money, even for household goods that will benefit the entire family. And now, to top it all off, stubby little Raymond, four years younger than I am, is allowed to drive the tractor. And I, I get to stump around after him, heaving bales onto that stupid flat sled we call a stoneboat, eating dust, parched and sweating.

I stop for a minute to pull a burr out of my socks. Thistles scratch me through my heavy plaid shirt, and my tongue sticks to the roof of my mouth.

"Come on, hurry up!" Raymond yells at me from his tractor seat. Proximity to mechanical power has gone right to his head. "Move it, Lynne's Lard Limited," bellows the tow-headed tyrant, heir to the farm, hurling his most hateful taunt.

As I slog through the stubble, enraged, I envision my future clearly: I will finish high school with top grades and I will get off this farm as fast as I can.

We are sprawled on the grass around the picnic table, slain by gluttony. We've dispatched the steak, the potato salad, the hot dogs and hamburgers, the lettuce salad, the bean salad, the dill and bean pickles and also a plate of fresh radishes, along with celery stuffed with Cheez Whiz. It's been a hot July weekend, and we are grateful for the evening shade.

It's the late 1970s, and my husband and I have driven from Lethbridge, Alberta, to visit my Saskatchewan family. Whenever we come home, my mother throws one of these gigantic family dinners, and we have "a gathering of the clan." Aside from all four of my siblings, a couple of my aunts and uncles are also here with their children, so it's general mayhem.

I'm sitting on a quilt (made by my mother) on the grass, playing with my brother Raymond's baby daughter, Leah. My husband loves my family's hubbub. He has only three living relatives in all of Canada: his mother, father and brother in Edmonton. He has just eaten an inordinate amount of food, and he sits in a green-and-white webbed lawn chair, smoking a cigar and shaking his foot, whether from nerves or boredom I do not know.

Even though we're all stuffed, my mother is pressing additional food on people. My middle sister is in university studying to be a social worker, my youngest brother is finishing high school, and our "baby sister" is six or seven. She is a tidy dynamo who rushes around with a dishrag in her fist, helping to clean up.

Suddenly we hear the grinding of gears as a vehicle turns in at the gate.

"That'll be Mervyn," my brother Ray allows.

"Trust him to come now," my mother adds.

Mervyn is my mother's only brother, a few years her junior. He lives three miles up the road, with my grandmother, Ada, on the farm that Grandpa Jack Burley, as family mythology has it, killed himself establishing. He died of a stroke one stiflingly hot day, shovelling wheat in one of his granaries.

My father and Mervyn have engaged in a feud for years, over a variety of issues ranging from broken fences to cattle prices. It's hard to know who's at fault and where the animosity began. When Raymond and I were kids, we spent a lot of time with my mother's parents, and looked up to Mervyn as our young uncle. Back then, we called him Uncle Mert and loved his teasing and his ever-ready gifts of chocolate bars and candy.

But Mert's in his late 40s now, and over the years he's become an increasingly sour and narrow-minded bachelor. He's a wiry man just over five feet tall, already wizened, with thinning brown hair that always looks dusty. His battered red Ford pickup shudders to a stop, and he bails out to regard all of us through narrowed eyes.

"Some folks sure live the life of Riley," he observes in his nasal drawl. This is a comment calculated to get my father's goat, of course, because Mervyn maintains no one works as hard or long as he does.

He crosses the grass and stands in front of me. As always, his overalls look too big for him and his boots are battered. "I figger you must be a mean little wench," he says.

"Mean? Who, me?"

"You weren't such a mean little gal, you'd have kids by now," he says, before stomping off toward the leftovers on the picnic table.

⚬From the narrow, open window above the bed, we can hear the noises from the Plaka outside, snatches of bouzouki music from the café around the corner, the pop of motor scooters, the steady thrum of tourism all around us. In the humid gloom of the bedroom, I feel a slight breath cross my thighs as he heaves himself off me, slapping my belly as he turns to sit up.

"There," he says. "I have maybe left you with good Greek baby."

Maybe he has, but the announcement leaves me feeling desolate.

"Why you cry?" he asks. "I come back tomorrow."

And when he does, if he does, I'll be gone, on the next ferry away from Crete, before either of us gets too comfortable.

I'm 34, turning 35 in August, and it's difficult for me to say if I am deafened or made more acute by the clichéd ticking of my biological clock. Divorce behind me, recovery from nervous breakdown tenuously under way, I have once again run away from the unbearable clarity of my "real" life to reinvent myself temporarily somewhere else. Spain and Mexico having failed in the past, this time I try Greece, a place I have always loved in the abstract, felt drawn to because of my ideas about its landscape and mythology.

As it turns out, I do love Greece in actuality, despite the lung-destroying cacophony of Athens, despite the difficulties of travelling alone, a blonde North American who speaks no Greek at all aside from a few pathetic phrase-book terms.

"I need to get away; I'm fed up with things here," I'd told friends as I left Edmonton. Once I arrive in Athens, a clinical clarity over-takes me. I am here to escape, yes, but my true mission is to get myself pregnant, by as much anonymous sex as necessary.

When I think about it for even a minute, I'm filled with an equal mixture of rage and pain about my marriage, about how and why it failed, and about my own guilty part in that dissolution. But I also am convinced (inchoately, inexplicably) that I need to become pregnant, and that I must do this as much as possible without a man, to somehow recoup the childless limbo of my married years. By this, I mean that I simply want a sperm donor. So, here, in the summer of 1983, despite a year of therapy, despite good antidepressants, I am as divorced from myself as I will ever be. I have taken all my North American neuroses to this ancient land, and I am on the prowl.

My nefarious mission is unwittingly aided by the Greek men themselves, who seem programmed to hit upon any and every foreign woman travelling alone. Doesn't matter what the woman does, what she says or how she looks: if she is travelling *sola*, she must be a slut and therefore available. While I resent this assumption, I'm simultaneously bemused that it serves my own selfish purposes.

My failure as a coquette is no handicap at all. This is how it works: at any point in the day, I take my stack of postcards, sit at a café and order a Greek coffee. I write a card or two, admire the view, absorb the passing scene. Within less than 30 minutes, the waiters will have flirted with me, and some total stranger will have approached me.

"German?" he will ask, displaying white teeth in a tanned face.

"*Nein*," I'll reply.

"Ah, American," he'll pounce.

"No, Canadian," I'll admit.

"Ah." A moment's cogitation. "Okay?" He gestures to the empty seat at my table, simultaneously signalling the waiter, who has been watching out of the corner of his eye. Two more coffees are on the way, and the rest of it is easy-peasy. Easy-sleazy.

I like to think that their machismo prevents my victims from suspecting they are being used. Although this sort of bare-bones mating is what I want, it's doing nothing positive for my morale. We part abruptly, each thinking less of the other, and I move on to a new city, a new island, new prey.

At the end of my three months abroad, I tot them all up: the baker, the teenage waiter, the engineer on Crete, the man on the motor scooter at the hotel on Patmos, the old man who never told me what he did... three of them were called Yorgos, or said they were. And after all that, nada. My uterus, not usually a jolly organ, has had the last laugh after all: I am still not pregnant.

Desperate times, long ago, and desperate measures. When I look back upon my younger self, I realize that my 30s represent my belated rebellion from all the roles I felt thrust upon me; they were the time when I enacted my rage about the unfairness of male and female roles. Compared to my life as a whole, you might even call those years an aberration, even though they seemed necessary to my hard-won understanding. I am chagrined by my actions now. And I am unspeakably thankful that no progeny resulted from my ill-conceived excursions.

Do I regret not having children? Some days yes, most days no. Will I die alone? Perhaps, but don't we all, I ask, existentialist-at-heart. Will I have "anything to show" for my life? Aha! To me, that's the bigger, more important question, one that only others can answer after I'm done. I admit that the older I get, the more provoked I am by people's unspoken assumptions about childless women. And I am impatient with myself for the years I spent feeling lesser because unchilded. I'm now of the Popeye Philosophy: "I yam what I yam." Flawed, fumbling still, I yam trying to be a decent human being, a principled teacher, a caring daughter, sister, aunt and friend and, most recently, a good man's wife. (I'll keep track of all those new babies' birthdays until I lose my marbles for good.) Most of all, in my remaining years, I want to be a more productive member of the larger society around me. That's my crop. I'll tend it the best way I'm able.

✑ Five months have passed since I began this essay with a Valentine's card; on my desk sits another letter, containing photographs taken just two weeks ago when almost all of my immediate family came to visit as I wed my long-time partner. One picture shows me, sitting on our deck, holding great-nephew Jaxton, who is an incredibly happy, still-bald baby. He wears a tiny red golf shirt, miniature blue jeans and fist-sized sneakers. I have my left hand on his back to support him; Jax has a fierce grip on my right forefinger. We're both looking to the left, at his mother, Leah, who's taking the picture; we're both smiling as hard as we can. Jax is drooling on my right wrist, and I don't mind at all.

Lynne Van Luven has been either a journalist or a teacher for the past 30-something years. She is the editor of *Going Some Place: Creative Non-Fiction Across Canada*, the first Canadian anthology of creative non-fiction ever published, and has taught journalism and non-fiction writing at the University of Victoria since 1997. She has a Ph.D. in Canadian literature and is Director of the Professional Writing Minor in Journalism and Publishing at the UVic's Department of Writing.

no grass widow

MARILYN DUMONT

In one ear I hear my mother telling me
She was a grass widow, that one.
In the other ear, I hear Elizabeth Brewster saying,
It's fine to be unmarried and childless
it's enough to be born and not give birth

I am woman enough
not some white-bread spinster
or uppity *mooniyawiskwew*
thinking she's too good for a poor man or a brown man

I'm no grass widow,
but I cut a path with a scythe as wide as my reach
and lace tall sheared stalks into baskets,
not for trinkets,
but to bear the weight
of wild wheat heads, millet, black rice,
and mashed berries that bleed into our stomachs
so we can eat for another day.

Marilyn Dumont's first collection of poetry, *A Really Good Brown Girl*, won the 1997 Gerald Lampert Memorial Award. This collection is in its 10th printing. Dumont's second book, *green girl dreams Mountains*, won the 2001 Stephan G. Stephansson Award. She teaches Aboriginal literature at the University of Alberta and creative writing through Athabasca University. She has a third manuscript with Kegedonce Press and is working on an exploration of Metis history, politics and identity through the figure of Gabriel Dumont.

acknowledgments

Thanks from the heart to all the contributors for their courage in sharing their experiences and to TouchWood Editions, especially Pat Touchie, for having faith in this anthology.